▥fastread

TIME MANAGEMENT

Get organized
and accomplish
more in less time

Bob Adams
and Lesley Bolton

Δ

Adams Media Corporation
Avon, Massachusetts

EDITORIAL
Publishing Director: Gary M. Krebs
Managing Editor: Kate McBride
Copy Chief: Laura MacLaughlin
Acquisitions Editor: Jill Alexander
Development Editor: Christel A. Shea

PRODUCTION
Production Director: Susan Beale
Production Manager: Michelle Roy Kelly
Series Designer: Daria Perreault
Cover Design: Paul Beatrice and Frank Rivera
Layout and Graphics: Brooke Camfield,
Colleen Cunningham, Michelle Roy Kelly
Daria Perreault

Published by Adams Media Corporation
57 Littlefield Street, Avon, MA 02322. U.S.A.
www.adamsmedia.com

ISBN: 1-58062-697-1

Printed in Canada.

J I H G F E D C B

Library of Congress Cataloging-in-Publication Data
Bolton, Lesley.
Fastread time management : get organized and accomplish more in less time /
Lesley Bolton.
p.   cm.
ISBN 1-58062-697-1
1. Time management. I. Title.
HD69.T54 B64 2002
640'.43--dc21
2002074484

This publication is designed to provide accurate and authoritative information with regard to the subject matter covered. It is sold with the understanding that the publisher is not engaged in rendering legal, accounting, or other professional advice. If legal advice or other expert assistance is required, the services of a competent professional person should be sought.

—From a *Declaration of Principles* jointly adopted
by a Committee of the American Bar Association
and a Committee of Publishers and Associations

Many of the designations used by manufacturers and sellers to distinguish their products are claimed as trademarks. Where those designations appear in this book and Adams Media was aware of a trademark claim, the designations have been printed in initial capital letters.

This book is available at quantity discounts for bulk purchases.
For information, call 1-800-872-5627

contents

chapter one 1
Assessing Your Relationship with Time
    Define "Time" 1
    Your Attitude Toward Time. 4
    Why Some Systems Don't Work 9
    Tracking Use of Time 12
    The Reality Factor. 15
    Learn to Prioritize 17

chapter two 19
Setting Priorities
    The To-Do List 19
    Create a Healthy To-Do List 20
    What Not to Do 24
    The Poorly Prepared List. 25

Know Your Terms. 27
The Dilemma of the Ringing Telephone 28
Important versus Urgent 29
The Four Categories. 29
Trivial versus Essential 30
The "Want to/Need to" Question 31
Is Time the Problem? 33
Where Did Time Go? 33

chapter three. 35
Accomplish More in Less Time
Know the Shortcuts. 35
The 80/20 Rule. 35
Multitasking: Pros and Cons. 38
The Costs of Multitasking. 41
Distractions 42
Interruptions 45
How to Delegate 47

chapter four. 51
You Set the Agenda
Working Effectively with Others 51
Just Three Little Words 52
The Golden Rule 54
Why Nice Guys Finish Last 54
Manage Meeting Black Holes 56
Recovering from Phone Addiction 57
Don't Be Bullied. 60

chapter five 61
Time Management for Managers
Tips for Dealing with Staff 61
Cutting Unproductive Meetings 64

Don't Waste Time with Indecision 66
Three Fears 67
Seven Tips for Making Decisions 70
Eliminating Mistakes 72

chapter six 75
Taming the Paper Tiger
Control the Paper Avalanche 75
Clutter Control 79
Incoming! 80
Organizing Your Work Space 82
Speed Writing 83
Write It Right—and Fast 84

chapter seven 89
Save Time Online
Know Your Resources 89
Online Job Search 90
Travel Made Simple 93
One-Stop Shopping 96
Online Education 96

chapter eight 99
Values-Based Time Management
What *Do* You Want? 99
Quality Time 100
Personal Prioritizing 100
The Values-Centered Life 102

chapter nine 105
Beating Stress
Stressless—Is That Even a Word? 105
Take Stock 107

Stress Less 108
Adjust to Achieve Balance 109
Maintain Methods of Healthy Living. 110
Set Up a Routine 111
Suit Yourself 113

index 115

Assessing Your Relationship with Time

Define "Time"

Time is one of the most versatile words in the English language. Consider all the different ways it's used: *hard time, keep time, it's about time, on time, closing time, time of year, double time, overtime, what time is it?* The list could go on until the *end of time*, but you get the point. Because time is not concretely defined, it is important to create your own definition in terms of your attitude and feelings toward it. Understanding "time" as it relates to you will take a great deal of reflection, but you cannot take a step forward until you know where you stand.

Establishing your relationship with time is an essential part of learning to use your time wisely. Everyone's relationship with time is different; therefore, all strategies for managing time will vary accordingly. It's not unlike buying a new pair of glasses. You must have an examination to determine your individual prescription.

1

Although you may be able to see fairly clearly with borrowed glasses, your vision is not as good as it could be. The same is true with time. If you are to reach your optimal level of time management, it must be tailored to you individually.

Your strengths, weaknesses, commitments, lifestyle, and responsibilities all play a role in the conception of a time management strategy. A person who fears time will need to create a time management system different from that of someone who challenges time. The system of someone with a spouse and children will differ from that of a person who has no dependents. Organizational systems, goals, and priorities will vary according to your personal tastes and mind-set. With each variance, the basic time management system will be altered to accommodate your individual needs.

Internal Time

Internal time is not nearly as concrete as external time. In fact, it is best described as a sense of time. Internal time is immeasurable; it is not comprised of minutes or days. It differs for every person and fluctuates with every activity. Because internal time is an abstract concept, it is difficult to give you a clear-cut definition. However, know that internal time changes. Its foundation lies in your thoughts, feelings, and actions; therefore, you do have control over this type of time.

Have you ever found yourself so engrossed in a project that you simply lost track of time? Did you feel a sense of timelessness? In that realm, you don't feel the limits or pressures set by external time. That freedom allows you to meet deadlines that at first seemed ridiculous. Surely there have been times when you were absolutely sure you would never accomplish certain things, but by some miracle you did. Focusing on the task, not the clock, allowed you to let go of external time and work solely on internal time.

Because of the limits imposed by external time, internal time is often ignored. However, it is in the realm of internal time that you are the most productive and creative. Nothing matters but what you are working on—"goals," "priorities," and "standards" as conscious factors fall by the wayside. You become so absorbed in what you're doing that external time does not exist.

In this world, it isn't possible to live only on internal time. Lives and schedules are coordinated on the basis of external time. But it is possible to work on internal time more often. Have you ever noticed how your degree of involvement in a project directly relates to the efficiency and quality of its completion? The more involved—committed—you are, the more likely you are to do a good job. As your degree of involvement increases, the project becomes more important to you, allowing internal time to play a greater role in the process. Involvement is the secret.

Tapping into your internal time reaps all kinds of benefits. Not only do you reach an optimal level of productivity and creativity, but also your stress levels go down. As timelessness alleviates pressure, the overall quality of your work will improve, relationships will be stronger, and you will find greater peace in your life.

External Time

Unlike internal time, which is conceptual, external time is concrete. It measures the duration of events and enables scheduling. External time is structured and constant, whether you are measuring hours, days, or years. Because it is a physical reality, external time is beyond your control.

How often do you look at your watch? People are constantly aware of time. In today's society, meetings, appointments, schedules, and deadlines drive personal and professional lives. You could lose your job, damage relationships, or miss opportunities if you disregard the clock. However, do not allow external time to govern your actions.

External time limits productivity, creativity, and well-being. Because this kind of time is structured and unchanging, there is a need to accomplish everything within time constraints, lest a fraction of a moment slips away. People make schedules revolving around rigid measurements. You estimate how long a task should take, and try to accomplish it within a predetermined number of minutes, hours, or days. Scheduling, or over scheduling, creates tension, anxiety, worry, and frustration—all for the sake of external time.

Watch the Time

External time is composed of a past, a present, and a future. The past is behind you, forever gone. The present is now, and all you have to work with at a given moment. The future represents possibility. If the present time isn't all it could be, there is always hope for the future. Although you are physically rooted in the present, mentally you are never in only one place. Being in too many places at one time opens the door for poor time management.

External time is not something you can disregard. It is always pressing against you, urging you on. You live within its bonds and abide by its rules. Without it your life would be chaotic. It is a necessary evil. Although you cannot change external time, you can learn to effectively adapt your way of life to coexist with it.

Your Attitude Toward Time

Even though time is set and cannot be changed, individual perceptions of time vary greatly. Before you can move forward in honing your time management skills, you must use a bit of what little time you have for self-reflection. Ask yourself the following questions:

- What time constraints did I experience growing up?
- How do I handle situations in which I am running late?
- Does it seem as though time is always working against me?
- Do I feel lost without my watch?
- Do I have leisure time?
- How well do I handle leisure time?
- Does time control me?
- How do I define "on time"? Early? To the second? Is half an hour late close enough?
- Is managing time a desperate act for me?

Answering these questions truthfully will uncover the underlying influences that have shaped your awareness of time. For example, if you grew up in a very organized and time-efficient atmosphere, your attitude toward time will be significantly different from that of someone who grew up in a random and disorganized environment. Perhaps your preconceived notions of time led you to create your own perception.

Though there are several attitudes you can take toward time, the following sections identify some of the most popular. Your transition into effective time management will be a lot smoother if you first determine why you need more control.

The Enemy

Many people see time as The Enemy. They feel that time is working against them; that no matter how hard they try to get it under control, they are always bested. Of course, that's a self-defeating and unrealistic attitude. Time is neither an enemy nor an ally. Time is simply there, a constant, and often a scapegoat. Because time will not (and cannot) bend to your will, you may think you are powerless in its grasp. However, if you *really* believed that, you wouldn't make the effort to get your time situation under control.

Quick Fix

Your first step toward time efficiency needs to be an adjustment of attitude. Take the blame for your ineffectual time management; then take control.

At Your Leisure

Some people value their leisure time but unknowingly abuse it. Often people will have a solid handle on their time management while working, but when it comes to play, they just aren't sure what to do with themselves. Leisure time can cause a well-organized and structured worker to panic.

Time isn't creating this tension; the lack of value recognition is. Those who fear leisure time may simply be afraid of wasting it. Ultimately, these people will do one of two things. They'll either fill their days and nights with work to eliminate the issue altogether, or they'll preserve their leisure time but do absolutely nothing with it.

Quick Fix

The same principles you use at work can be applied to your leisure time. If you manage your time well at work, you obviously have a system set up pertaining to the demands of your work. You have prioritized, set goals, and found a balance between what is important and what is urgent (as clarified in Chapter 2). All you have to do is apply those same standards to your leisure time.

A Fear of Work Time

Some people take the opposite approach, valuing their leisure time but fearing work. These people also believe that time takes on different standards of measurement. Quite often they aren't happy with their jobs or feel as though work is something that is forced on them. They will subconsciously, or sometimes blatantly, create a resistance. Their leisure time is spent in a fulfilling manner while their work time is spent in chaos, accomplishing very little. They consider time spent working to be time taken away from their lives, thereby rejecting or neglecting what they really value.

With this approach, time will pass quickly when spent in leisure activities but stand still while at work. Again, an attitude adjustment is required. You can still find leisure preferable to work, but if you have a better outlook toward your work, time won't seem to take on such different proportions.

Quick Fix

Analyze what enables you to make the most of your leisure time and apply that to your time at work. The situation, values, and goals will be different within each area, but if you employ the basics, you will be on your way.

Perpetually Late

There are some people who make a habit of being late to everything—social functions, work, and appointments. Many of you will have developed a reputation for being late. While you may be displeased with this reputation, it does serve as an excuse, and others may come to accept it. But it *can* backfire. Those who are continually late may find themselves stuck in a rut of constant tardiness once it becomes expected (and accepted) of them.

There are also those who are late only in certain aspects of their lives. For example, someone may be consistently on time for work (sometimes even early) but always late for social and family functions, or vice versa. Quite often it can be the sense of responsibility or fear that determines arrival time. Regarding the above example, this person may feel a stronger sense of responsibility toward his employer as far as time is concerned and is therefore driven to be punctual. Family and friends will likely be more accepting of his tardiness, so the repercussions will not be as severe.

Whether there are repercussions or not, consistent tardiness shows disrespect for other people. You may also miss out on opportunities to take on additional responsibilities as others come to learn that they cannot rely on you.

Quick Fix

There are a few things you can do to try to curb your habit. For instance, you can trick yourself by setting your clocks forward a bit. Or plan to be at your destination fifteen minutes before you are expected—if you are normally fifteen minutes late, this should get you there right on time. Also try scheduling at least ten minutes of downtime between appointments or activities. Ultimately, your determination to develop an effective time management system will carry you even further.

Disregarding Time

Finally, there are some people out there who simply have no regard for time. You may think this is an ideal way to live your life, but it can create just as many problems as believing time is your enemy. If you have no sense of time, you have no guidelines for accomplishing things. *Goal* is a foreign word to you, and deadlines don't exist. Basically, you have set yourself apart from the one thing the world has in common.

If you constantly resist the idea of time, you are giving it continuous play. Considering that you have to acknowledge that it exists, you cannot escape it entirely. Time is not something that can be ignored for long. This is not to say that you should obsess about it, but at least try to recognize its effects on you and take control.

Why Some Systems Don't Work

Time management systems are like diets. First, they are both common items on New Year's resolution lists. Second, people often dive into both with the greatest of intentions, only to slowly lose interest until the goal is entirely forgotten. Lastly, both work for a little while, but eventually the weight and the chaos slowly creep back into your life.

How do you create a time management system that works once and for all? What makes this system any better than all the others available? The secret lies in the balance between the two types of perceptual time. Most time management systems focus on only external time. They don't offer the possibility that time awareness can ever leave the psyche. There are also a few systems that focus on only internal time. These simply won't work because it is a fact that our lives are affected by external time.

You must discover how you relate to time, then learn and apply new skills to achieve the best possible time management system. If you are unaware of how you view time, your feelings toward it, and the preconceived notions you have regarding it, your skills may work for a while, but eventually you may find that you have fallen back into your old patterns. The system in this book involves the reconstruction of not only your time habits, but also your overall relationship with time, allowing you access to higher levels of performance, satisfaction, and peace.

Because discovering your relationship with time must be done with self-reflection, there is little to do but try to get you started. Prior sections raised several points for you to consider. Try to keep your discoveries in mind while reading the rest of this book, because from here on out you will deal with only external time. Remember: To make your time management system work at its optimum level, you will need to incorporate both types of time.

What Are the Setbacks?

What is holding you back and what is working against you? Take a step back and try to look at your life objectively. Are there recurring factors in your life that won't allow you to get ahead? If you are like most, there are several small details that can add up to big problems. You may or may not realize what these setbacks are. Ask yourself the following questions:

- Do you try to fit a double workload into a single day more than once a week?
- Do you have difficulty saying no to a request for your time?
- Are your goals and aspirations unrealistic?
- Do you have a tendency to procrastinate?
- Do you daydream often?
- Do you own a wide variety of personal organizers? Or none at all?
- Do you take pleasure in your work?
- Is your day filled with matters that must be attended to right away?
- Do you show symptoms of perfectionism?
- Are you swimming in sticky notes?
- Do you rush around the house while your family enjoys their leisure time?
- Do you often have more than two things going on at once?

- Do you have a tendency to lose things?
- Do you enjoy starting projects but have difficulty completing them?

The Root of the Problem

Chances are, you will have answered yes to at least one of the above questions, maybe even several. The answers aren't important here; what is important is the degree of awareness you have achieved. Consider the reasons behind the yes answers; take a moment to analyze why it is you feel you daydream, or why you lose things. The reasons behind the actions are what you need to understand and address. You cannot defeat a problem without first getting to its root.

If you answered no to all questions, don't assume you are in the clear. If you are concerned about your time management skills, there must be a problem somewhere. It may be necessary to dig deeper into your daily schedule and nitpick all details before you are able to discover what has been tripping you up. Perhaps you have formed habits you weren't even aware of. Again, take a look at those important activities you never seem to get to. Consider why you have chosen these items to push aside for later. What sorts of things stand in the way of your accomplishing the important? Try to be as specific as possible.

Know Where to Begin

Keep in mind that this exercise isn't designed to help you place blame. Rather, it is intended to help you give reason to your hectic life. Once you discover the areas that need the most attention, you will be able to work efficiently on your time management skills. Don't feel bad if it seems as though your entire life needs to be worked on; that feeling is actually quite common.

Time is not the issue here, your use of time is. You have to take control and adapt your life to work within the time you are allotted. Depending on your degree of desperation, it may take a couple of hours or a couple of months to fix all of your time management concerns. It may cost you time up front, but developing good time management skills will reduce stress and enable you to work better and accomplish more.

Tracking Use of Time

You understand that time is constant; it cannot be changed to fit your needs or anyone else's. You all have a certain amount of time allotted to you, but how you choose to use that time varies widely. To be successful in time management, you must first take a look at how you presently use the time you have.

Time Log

Keep a record of each activity you participate in within a twenty-four-hour period of time. Yes, this will take away from the time you have, and you may even feel it is necessary to record how much time you spent recording activities. But this is a relatively easy way to get a good look at your time habits and how many of those are wasteful.

Create three columns on a piece of paper. Title the first column "Time Began." You will record, to the minute, what time you begin an activity. The second column will simply be "Activity." It is a good idea to add detail to your entries in this column. For instance, instead of simply saying, "exercised," you could specify jogging and give the total distance you ran. The third column will be "Time Ended." Again, you need to record the time exactly. An optional fourth column is titled "Completed." This is useful for tasks that are part of your to-do list. However, since this exercise is meant only to track your time, the "Completed" column is optional.

Time Log

Time Began	Activity	Time Ended	Completed
5:45 A.M.	Alarm clock goes off— 15 minutes of snooze time	6:00 A.M.	√
6:00 A.M.	Dress, start coffee, stretch	6:20 A.M.	
6:20 A.M.	Jogging	7:05 A.M.	√
7:05 A.M.	Shower	7:20 A.M.	
7:20 A.M.	Dress, hair, makeup, etc.	8:00 A.M.	√
8:00 A.M.	Coffee, breakfast, morning paper	8:30 A.M.	—
8:30 A.M.	Commute to work	9:00 A.M.	
9:00 A.M.	* Greet fellow employees * Answer voice mail and e-mail * Check planner for daily schedule	9:30 A.M.	— √ —
9:30 A.M.	Organize desk, final preparation for meeting	9:40 A.M.	
9:40 A.M.	Personal phone call	9:50 A.M.	√—left msg
9:50 A.M.	Use restroom, refill coffee, head to conference room	10:00 A.M.	
10:00 A.M.	Meeting with VP and marketing	11:30 A.M.	√—Revisions due next Tues.
11:30 A.M.	Downtime—talk with fellow employees, refresh in restroom, relax	12:00 P.M.	
12:00 P.M.	Walk to deli	12:10 P.M.	
12:10 P.M.	Lunch and gossip with coworkers	12:50 P.M.	
12:50 P.M.	Walk back to work	1:00 P.M.	
1:00 P.M.	Paperwork/research	1:50 P.M.	√
1:50 P.M.	Chat with coworker	2:05 P.M.	
2:05 P.M.	Paperwork/research	2:45 P.M.	

Time Log
(continued)

Time Began	Activity	Time Ended	Completed
2:45 P.M.	Outline proposal	3:00 P.M.	√
3:00 P.M.	Write proposal	3:05 P.M.	√
3:05 P.M.	Personal phone call	3:15 P.M.	—
3:15 P.M.	Coffee, restroom break, chat with coworkers	3:35 P.M.	
3:35 P.M.	Write proposal	4:40 P.M.	√—Finish Intro/Appendix
4:40 P.M.	Break	4:50 P.M.	
4:50 P.M.	Clean desk, organize things for tomorrow	5:05 P.M.	
5:05 P.M.	Commute	5:30 P.M.	
5:30 P.M.	Post office	5:45 P.M.	√
5:45 P.M.	Driving	6:00 P.M.	
6:00 P.M.	Grocery shopping	6:35 P.M.	
6:35 P.M.	Drive home	6:50 P.M.	
6:50 P.M.	Unwind, look through mail	7:10 P.M.	
7:10 P.M.	Prepare/eat/clean up dinner	8:00 P.M.	
8:00 P.M.	Phone calls to friends	8:30 P.M.	
8:30 P.M.	Drive to Laundromat	8:40 P.M.	X—get soap!
8:40 P.M.	Laundry, read magazine	9:40 P.M.	
9:40 P.M.	Drive home	9:50 P.M.	
9:50 P.M.	Drop laundry—collapse on couch in front of TV	11:00 P.M.	
11:00 P.M.	Wash up, go to bed		

Keep in mind that every minute needs to be accounted for. Try to be as specific as possible. The more specific, the better you will be able to calculate how your time is spent. For example, be more specific than just recording "work." Break it down into specific tasks, even if they aren't completed. Also take note of all interruptions, distractions, and breaks. At the end of the day, calculate how much time was productive and how much was wasted. (Breaks do not count as a waste of time.)

Record Your Findings

Grouping your findings into categories such as "Productive" and "Wasteful" will work just fine. However, you may want to break them down even further into subcategories such as "Interruptions," "Breaks," "Family Time," "Work Time," "Complete Waste of Time"—you get the picture. Divide them up into areas that are important to you. You may be surprised to find that you accomplish more than you thought. On the other hand, you may find that you waste more time than you use productively.

Now that you have an idea of where your time is going, you can begin to plan your strategy. Pay special attention to areas that are in desperate need of attention, and what you're doing right in the areas that seem to work well for you.

Don't throw your log away. In a few weeks, you may want to repeat this exercise and take a look at how the two compare. By then, you should be showing some progress. If not, you will want to re-evaluate your strategy.

Quick Fix

Make a habit of keeping a time log once a month. You will remain constantly updated on the progress you make with your time management system.

The Reality Factor

Let's face it, dreams of time management aren't always going to end up with a happily-ever-after ending. You live in the real world, and must take that into consideration. Reality has a way of altering even the most carefully laid plans. The best way to curb the disruption that may result is to be as prepared as possible.

Granted, you can be prepared for only so much. However, as long as you accept the possibility of a setback, you are further ahead than you may think. As you begin to analyze your use of time and how to make the most of it, pencil in interruptions on your plan. By allowing for interruptions, whether there is an emergency situation or an unexpected call, flexibility will preserve your schedule.

Time Estimations

Reality hits full force when you set outrageous goals and expect to get things done in less time than they should take. First, you are going to do a poor job by rushing through the early items on your list. Then, the rest of your list is going to get backed up and may lead to even more delays due to missed calls and connections, and a lack of confidence.

Some people recommend scheduling twice the amount of time a task should take. Then you will almost always come out ahead. If this plan of action appeals to you, by all means set it in motion. However, consider that this strategy could also backfire. What happens when you finish the report in less than half the time you anticipated? The next item on your list is a lunch date that won't take place for another hour. What are you going to do now? Of course there are always other things to be done. Don't be so in awe of the spare time you have that you simply do nothing, wasting time that could have been put to good use.

Life's Surprises

There are some things you simply cannot anticipate. Remember that your plan for time management is just that: a plan. It isn't a strict code you must obey at all times, nor is it the ruling force for your life. It is simply a guideline to help you optimize your resources, and accomplish what you want to and need to without sacrificing fun and spontaneity.

Learn to Prioritize

So now that you are all geared up and ready to dive headfirst into the time management mélange called life, where do you start? Before you do anything else, you need to set your priorities. What do you need? What do you want? Where do you want to be? There are a thousand questions you can ask yourself, but what it all boils down to is finding out what is most important to you.

Priorities can be classified in several different ways. For example, you will have a different set of priorities at work than you will at home. However, for the time being, look at your life in general. Encompassing all of these different divisions, brainstorm everything that is important to you. Your list may be long or have only a few key items on it. Either way is fine; just remember to be honest with yourself.

Once you have a list compiled, pull out the top ten items that have the most significance to you. *Don't toss the rest;* you may want to use them later for other lists or to reevaluate this one. Rank your top ten accordingly, with number one being the highest priority. This is for your eyes only, so no one else is going to see that you rate caring for your dog as a higher priority than your friends. If you have difficulty ranking one item over another, don't spend too much time on it now. This list is by no means set in stone. In fact, you will continually reevaluate and restructure your personal and professional priorities as you proceed throughout life.

Once you have a tangible list of what you hold dear, refer to it often. Keep it handy so when a question of how you will spend your time arises, you will have a guide pointing you in the right direction. Don't hesitate to make changes; it is to be expected.

This is not the only time you will be asked to prioritize. Establishing priorities is the key to effective time management, so it is essential that you learn to do it well now and form a good basis for the future.

Quick Fix

It is essential that you take time with this first step and get it right. Unless you have a list of priorities, you will never be able to assess how far and how well you have progressed.

chapter two

Setting Priorities

The To-Do List

There's nothing new about the to-do list. Folks have been jotting down lists of things they need to do, and then checking each item off the list as they do it, for a long time. The more you need to do, and the more pressure you feel to do it, the more helpful keeping a list can be.

The List from Hell

We'll impose a midlevel of organization—not quite a minute-by-minute script, but more than a simple list of tasks.

To Do Before Work
- Exercise: one hundred sit-ups, fifty push-ups, twenty-five squats
- Review agenda and materials for staff meeting

- Read *The Wall Street Journal*
- Morning commute (seventeen minutes)
- Listen to motivational self-help tape on time management

Morning
- Answer faxes, overnight mail, voice mail, e-mail (8:00–9:00)
- Staff meeting (9:00–10:30)
- Organize research for quarterly report (10:30–11:45)
- Drive to lunch meeting (fifteen minutes)
- Lunch meeting (noon–1:30)

Afternoon
- Write draft of quarterly report (1:30–3:00)
- Meet with committee on workplace expectations (3:00–4:40)
- Afternoon commute (eighteen minutes; pick up dry-cleaning)

    That's it. There's your workday, all laid out. But do all that, and you'll likely be laid out, too.

Create a Healthy To-Do List

Priorities and organization are important because they keep you focused. Remember, however, that tools should make your life easier and smoother. The following hints will help you stay on track *and* stay sane.

    1. **Don't jam the list.** Master this one, and everything else falls into place.
        Be realistic in your expectations and your time

estimates. Make a real-world list, not an itinerary for fantasyland. Otherwise, you'll spend the day running late, running scared, and possibly just flat-out running to catch up. You won't even have time to notice how your efficiency drops as you become cranky and exhausted.

If by some miracle things take less time than you had allowed for, rejoice! You've given yourself the gift of found time, yours to spend however you want and need to.

To help follow rule 1, follow rule 2.

2. **Air it out.** Overestimate the commute time—allowing for the dawdler in the fast lane and the cautious car at the left-turn arrow. Factor in the wait before the meeting, the line at lunch, and the time spent bouncing around in voice-mail limbo.

3. **List possibilities, not imperatives.** Your frame of mind when you make the list is as important as the specific items on the list itself. You're listing tasks that you hope, want, and usually need to finish during the day. You're not, however, creating a blueprint for the rest of the universe.

Suppose you're sick enough to have to stay flat on your back in bed for two days, and you can barely wobble around the house in bathrobe and slippers on the third. In all, you miss an entire week of work.

Meanwhile, what happened to the stuff on your to-do list?

The meetings went on without you. Folks figured out they could live without the quarterly report for another week. You've got 138 unheard messages on the voice mail (62 of them from the same person); 178 items in the e-mail box (52 of them the result of a list server getting "stuck" and sending out the same message multiple times); and a desk awash in memos, faxes, overnight letters, and other unnatural disasters. You take stuff home for a week, trying to get caught up.

That's bad, but it isn't that bad. Western civilization did not grind to a halt. Commerce and government managed to struggle on without you. It's too late to respond to some of those urgent memos and messages, but it turns out they really didn't need a response after all.

Try to remember that the next time you're relatively healthy but nevertheless falling behind on the day's tasks. What you do *is* important, but everyone needs to keep things in proper perspective.

4. **Don't carve the list on stone tablets.** Your list has to be flexible if it's going to do you any good. You have to be able to change it, digress from it, flip it on its ear, add to it, or wad it up and toss it into the recycle bin if that is what's really going to help.

   Don't try to fit a format; find or create a method that fits you. If you like an intricate grid system, with squares for every five minutes during the day, go for the grid. If crayon on butcher paper is more your style, then scrawl away.

5. **Order creatively.** Vary your pace, alternating difficult and easy, long and short, jobs requiring creative thought with rote functions. Change activities often enough to keep fresh.

   Make sure the most important tasks get done before you drown in a sea of relative trivia. Answer the e-mail first if it's the top priority on your list. If it isn't, schedule it for later in the day. Don't do it first simply because it's there, demanding attention or because it's relatively easy or because you've gotten in the habit of doing it first.

   Attack mentally taxing jobs when you're most alert and energetic.

6. **Break the boulders into pebbles.** So you have boxed off an entire afternoon to "Do newsletter." You carefully counted backward from the publication date to allow for printing and mailing, and allowed four hours to write and edit the material and lay it out.

   Ah-ha! Folks didn't get their copy in on time. You didn't get yours written on time, either. The first page layout vanished into the ether. The longer and later you struggled, the deeper into the mire you sank. And when you finally finished, the newsletter was a mess, and so were you.

   Now, you schedule several sessions, one to write, edit, and lay out; and another to select and edit reader letters. You let the finished pages sit and cool off for at least a day, do a final read through, and send it to the printer.

   The newsletter *and* its editor come out in much better shape.

7. **Schedule breaks, time-outs, and little rewards.** Many of you schedule "rest" last, if you schedule it at all. By the time you get to it—if you get to it—it's too late to do you any good.

   If you don't put rest on the list, you won't rest. Plan the break for when it will do you the most good—before you become too tense or exhausted. Brief rests at the right times will help you maintain a steady, efficient pace.

   You may just want (and need) to schedule a game of catch with your child or a walk around the neighborhood with your spouse.

   Yes, that may sound awful. Instead of dwelling on that, start planning a balanced, fulfilling life.

8. **Set long-range *and* short-range goals.** You know you should do some serious financial planning. You know you should have a current will. You know you should

create a systematic plan for home maintenance and repair.

If you know all that and never seem to get to it—put it on the schedule.

9. **Be ready to abandon the list.** "If you only write the story that is planned," writer and teacher Ellen Hunnicutt tells her students, "you miss the story that is revealed."

The same goes for the story of your life. The most important things you do probably never appear on any to-do list or show up on the day planner. Never become so well organized and so scheduled that you stop being alert to life's possibilities—the chance encounter or the sudden inspiration.

10. **You don't have to make a list at all.** The to-do list is a tool. Techniques for creating an effective list are suggestions, not commandments. If they help, follow them—adapting and modifying them to fit your own circumstances and inclinations. If they don't help, make your own kind of list, or don't make any list at all.

What Not to Do

Along with noting and organizing the tasks you'll do, you might also want to write down those things you *won't* do.

Not-to-dos don't include the sort of epic life-pledges that appear on New Year's resolution lists, like: stop smoking, don't nag, and cut out chocolate and caffeine. (Although you can certainly make that kind of list if you find it helpful!) Consider instead day-to-day tasks that have fallen to you by custom, habit, or lot but that should properly be done by someone else (or not done at all).

Examine large tasks (serving on the school board) and small ones (responding to every memo from the district supervisor) to make sure (1) they need to be done and (2) you're the one who needs to do them. If the task fails on either count, put it on the not-to-do list.

The Poorly Prepared List

It's true—The List has a dark side. Keep in mind that the following issues are only the consequences of not creating a healthy and sound to-do list. A bad list has the power to destroy your self-esteem. If you are continually unable to complete even a fraction of the items found on your list, you may begin to think of yourself as a failure. It can make your life even more hectic than it was before. You may neglect the important things in favor of the small urgencies. Your stress level could rise, affecting your eating and sleeping habits. In short, the list could make you its slave.

It is extremely important that you are careful in preparing your to-do list, but fear not. Once you finish with this section you will be in control and ready to conquer.

Good versus Bad

Realistic To-Do List		Fantasyland To-Do List	
Call Michael	☐	End world hunger	☐
Schedule meeting with Cheryl	☐	Start a business	☐
Call insurance agent	☒	Run a coast-to-coast race	☐
Work on resume	☐	Hand wash all laundry	☐
Get a haircut	☒	Rebuild the car engine	☐
Return mother-in-law's phone call	☐	Write a book	☐
Pick up fresh fruit at the market	☐	Build addition	☐
Drop off clothes at dry cleaners	☒	Climb Mount Everest	☐
Schedule doctor's appointment	☐	Lose 50 pounds	☐

Are You Ready?

First, you need to relax. Don't allow your brain to overload with ideas of what needs to be done. Clear your mind of any future activities aside from those belonging to the day ahead. Focus on only what needs to be accomplished today.

Begin by writing down the urgencies. These are probably foremost in your mind anyway. Next are the important items. Consider also the want-to-do items. A day filled with constant need-tos and should-dos will exhaust you pretty quickly. However, you do not want to go overboard with items added. Once you are pleased with the list you've created, estimate a time allowance for each item. It is a good idea to overestimate a bit. This will give you a cushion.

Rank each item according to its precedence. Don't stress yourself out—keep it simple. The list shouldn't itemize too many activities, but it also shouldn't itemize too few. "Simple" does not mean sloppy and slacking, but rather clear and precise. If you have to second-guess the list regularly, it isn't doing you much good.

Bear in mind that this list is not set in stone. As a list of *ideas* and *possibilities* for a run of the day's activities, it can, and most likely will, change. It will be difficult to change a list that is complicated and full of intricate detail, so simplicity will take you a long way.

Do not rank everything number one. Your list should reflect reality. The consequences and ill effects mentioned earlier are mostly due to the refusal to incorporate reality into the list. Do not overburden yourself with a thousand activities that need to be completed. Most importantly, don't plan to cram activities back-to-back. You will need a break, and not everything will go as planned—that is guaranteed.

Be realistic about your expectations. Estimating time is another factor people often find difficult. You may think you are superhuman at times. What would normally take someone an hour will take you only half an hour because you know a shortcut, or you expect a surge of energy to hit about that time.

Keep the list accessible. Even if you are prudent in your list preparation, and take the time to carefully evaluate every item in terms of importance, your list will not do you a bit of good if you leave it lying on the kitchen counter. This may go without saying, but more often than you think, lists are composed on a scrap of paper only to be thrown away minutes later by an unaware passerby. Or perhaps you are so absorbed in your list that you forget to write down "carry list on person at all times."

Things do happen. That's why it is important to write your list somewhere easily accessible. For instance, most paper and electronic planners have a place designated specifically for to-do lists. Or you may have your own system that works better. Regardless of where you choose to keep your list, it needs to be with you at all times.

The to-do list is the foundation of a perfect schedule, and scheduling is the next step in getting your life in order. Although many believe the schedule to be the forefather of time management, until you master the to-do list, you will be unable to complete your transition from a time captive to a time commander.

Know Your Terms

The differences between "important" and "urgent" are subtle, but understanding them will make prioritizing that much easier. Think of things that are important to you: your family, your friends, your career, your future. They are basic motivations that drive and guide your life.

Now consider urgencies: a ringing doorbell or telephone, a beeping pager, an e-mail from your superior saying that he needs to see you "now." Urgencies demand immediate attention.

The next several sections will elaborate upon the "Important versus Urgent" questions, the choices and decisions you must make, and how those choices will affect your priorities, your time, and your management of both.

The Dilemma of the Ringing Telephone

Spend a little time now to save a lot of time later. Devote conscious thought to everyday choices you may not be thinking about now. The more uncomfortable you are with this exercise, the more potential it has to help you.

Imagine for a moment that you work in an office and that your office has a telephone (not too much of a stretch there). The phone rings. Will you answer it? Believe it or not, you do have a choice (especially if you have voice mail or can let the call ring through to another person), although most people automatically snatch up a ringing phone. (Remember Pavlov and his salivating dogs?)

You usually have to make the decision to answer a ringing telephone without the most important piece of information, namely, who's on the other end. Certainly there's an urgency. Your phone is there. On your desk. Ringing. Repeatedly. And it *could* be important—your child's school, your spouse, your parent. It could also be an associate wondering if you're participating in the office football pool.

On second thought, maybe it's just as well you can't always know who's calling and what they're calling about.

Important versus Urgent

To become a savvy time manager, you need to understand the difference, and act on it.

For example, if the health and safety of a loved one were at stake (or at least seemed to be, and there's no way you'd take a chance with something like that), the situation would demand immediate action. A challenge that is both important and urgent demands a lot from you, but it doesn't require any decision making—it immediately becomes your top priority.

On the other hand, a call from your financial planner regarding your toddler's education fund is also clearly important but lacks a sense of urgency. (Why do you have to deal with that now?) Be careful—priorities like this seem to be on your list permanently. It's okay to skip the call now, but be committed to calling back. This might be a good time to gather key paperwork, make a list of pending issues, and set aside a chunk of time to resolve several outstanding financial questions.

Quick Fix

Take the time to sort out your personal and professional goals and responsibilities, ultimately understanding the distinction between important and urgent.

The Four Categories

Once you understand what "urgent" and "important" mean to you, you'll be in a better position to look at calls and tasks with some perspective. To help you sort out your responsibilities and demands on your time, consider the following categories:

1. Urgent and important: relates to your core values and needs immediate attention.

2. Important but not urgent: no sense of immediacy.
3. Urgent but not important: doesn't touch core values.
4. Neither important nor urgent: everything else.

Here are a few samples to help you sort:

Urgent and Important
- Call from day care—your child is sick
- Big presentation to make in two hours
- Car swerves in front of you

Important but Not Urgent
- Regular exercise
- Long-range financial planning
- "Quality" time with family

Urgent but Not Important
- Colleague needs to talk with you "right away"
- Concert tickets went on sale four minutes ago
- E-mail icon is blinking

Neither Important nor Urgent
- Working a crossword puzzle
- Catching up on office gossip
- Reading the baseball box scores

There really is an important, maybe even urgent, point to all this. Take a look at the two categories "important but not urgent" and "urgent but not important." You might be doing too much of latter.

Trivial versus Essential

Life is full of urgencies that really don't make any difference in the long run (or even in the short run, for that matter). Yes, you're four minutes late for that department meeting. But the department meeting is a fat waste of everybody's time (including the person running it), ninety minutes of plodding through announcements you could have read for yourself (or chosen to ignore).

Getting to that meeting is now urgent but not particularly important.

Technology has increased the sense of urgency, in the workplace, especially. An overnight letter cries for more immediate attention than something sent bulk rate or even first class. A fax shouts louder than an overnight letter. E-mail screams above them all.

But the delivery system has no bearing on the importance of the content. That e-mail message may be no more important to you than the letter informing you that "YOU MAY ALREADY BE A WINNER!" in the big sweepstakes.

You also have extremely important choices that don't carry with them any sense of urgency. Of course you should exercise regularly. You know it's good for you, mentally as well as physically. You'll do it. You absolutely will. Just not right now. Hey, you're four minutes late for the department meeting.

Quick Fix

Take conscious control of your decision making. Do you respond to the urgent, even if it's relatively unimportant, and shun the important, unless it also carries a sense of urgency? Reevaluate your to-do list, keeping your goals and values in mind, and prioritize accordingly.

The "Want to/Need to" Question

If all this business of dividing activities into four quadrants on an important/urgent grid seems like a lot of work, here's an easier way to begin to gain control of your daily life.

Again, you're going to need to develop a way to interrupt yourself several times a day. These interruptions can coincide with your minibreaks, but they don't have to.

Simply stop what you're doing, take a breath, and ask yourself the following question:

"Is this what I want or need to be doing right now?"

You can, of course, modify the question to fit your own circumstances and your approach to life. The following version is a modification of the "Lakein Question" proposed by Alan Lakein in his book, *How to Get Control of Your Time and Your Life* (1996). However you change the question, be sure to touch on the three key elements:

Is this what I *want* . . .

. . . or *need* . . .

. . . to be doing *right now*?

Note that it's *or,* not *and.* Obviously, a task can be a long way from what you'd really like to be doing and still be the thing you need to do.

If you answer yes, go back to what you were doing. You'll have affirmed your choice of activities and made your decision consciously, a key element in successful time management.

If you want or need to do it but not right now, put it off and do something with a higher degree of urgency. That way, you'll avoid getting caught in deadline pressure later.

If you neither want nor need to be doing it, now or ever, stop.

It may seem amazing to you, but if you stick with the "want/need" question for twenty-one days, you'll catch yourself doing things you can't justify, and you'll be able to shift your focus to better serve your needs.

Quick Fix

Several times a day, ask yourself, "Is this what I want or need to be doing right now?" Your answer will help you keep your priorities in perspective and you can manage your time accordingly.

Is Time the Problem?

Time management isn't always a matter of time at all.

For some people, going to a department meeting and sitting in a passive stupor is neither important nor particularly pleasurable (unless you're a gifted daydreamer), but it is a lot *easier* than exercising. For others, confronting the office deadline may be a lot easier than trying to iron out the kinks in a relationship. Often, people take the path of least resistance, especially if they can justify the choice on grounds other than ease. ("I *have* to go to the meeting. It's my job.")

Other times, people don't do things because they're difficult or they make them uncomfortable. Rather than being honest, people use the convenient excuse of not having enough time. Improving your time management skills won't make these problems go away. You have to uncover the real cause of your failure to act, then choose to act despite your fear or reluctance.

Where Did Time Go?

Time needs "managing" only because there doesn't seem to be enough time to do everything you want or need to do. In particular, you may never seem able to find time for those important but not urgent activities.

Stop looking. You'll never *find* time. It isn't lost. You're living it, and you have to consciously decide to live it in certain ways and not others. You have to *make* time by taking it away from one activity and giving it to another.

Conscientious and creative use of the to-do list can help here. If you want to exercise three times a week, if you need to do some long-range career and financial planning, or if you care enough about another human being to want to nurture your relationship, you will schedule time for these things. Otherwise, you may not get to them, and even if you do, you'll give them only your leftover time, when energy and focus are at their lowest.

You can also create time for yourself by slicing some of that "urgent but not important (or even a lick of fun)" stuff out. Upcoming chapters will propose ways to do just that.

chapter three

Accomplish More in Less Time

Know the Shortcuts

Now that you know what you want to achieve and have begun your journey, undoubtedly you are eager to begin saving that precious commodity called time. Learn how to pass off jobs you never wanted to do in the first place. Consider both the pros and cons of multitasking and whether it is right for you. The theories in this chapter, as in the rest of the book, will work best when modified to suit your needs and your style.

The 80/20 Rule

Everyone has heard of the 80/20 Rule in one variation or another. It is also known as Pareto's Principal and The Vital Few. The rule states that 80 percent of your results will come from 20 percent of your efforts, which also means that 20 percent of your results will come from 80 percent of your efforts. Vilfredo Pareto, an Italian economist, developed this principle when he discovered that 80 percent of the wealth of England belonged to 20 percent of the population. Upon further study of different countries and different time periods, he found that this equation became a pattern applied to all examples put forth.

Since his discovery, several people have applied the rule to nearly all aspects of life and found that it fits quite nicely. For instance:

- 20 percent of your clothes are worn 80 percent of the time.
- 80 percent of a store's sales comes from 20 percent of its customers.
- 20 percent of motorists cause 80 percent of automobile accidents.
- 20 percent of acreage will produce 80 percent of the crop.
- 20 percent of companies within an industry will conduct 80 percent of the business of that industry.

Though it can be a rather discouraging statement, it is a good guideline to use while examining your management of time. The problem with the 80/20 Rule is that for most aspects of your life, you don't know which is the 20 percent until after the fact. Therefore, it does very little good to take the time to analyze the rule. But as far as time management is concerned, examining this rule and its effect on your life will help you to spend your time more wisely.

Assign a Value Scale

To make the 80/20 Rule work for you, first assign a scale of value to your different activities. When you consider time well spent, what is it you have accomplished? This value scale will vary from person to person. Some may place highest value on financial security, while others regard health as their top priority. The values themselves will also vary as you go through life. What takes precedence now may not even be an issue later on.

Keep an Activity Log

An easy way to assess how well you use your time is to keep an activity log. For each activity entry, record how long you worked, whether or not the task was completed, and rank it according to its place on your value scale. At the end of the day, take a look at how many activities are ranked number one and how much time you spent with each. Chances are, in comparison to the rest of the day, very little time was spent on the "valued activities"—those that will produce the most positive results. If this happens to be the case, you have fallen under the 80/20 spell. But that's okay; it is to be expected.

Now, take a look at those activities that ranked lowest on your scale. All those little chores that get in the way of your life are often *should-dos*. These can be terribly annoying because you know they are things that need to be done but really have very little impact on your happiness and satisfaction. The should-dos are usually put off until they become urgent, which throws your plan for time management right out the window.

See if you have any alternative means of accomplishing these tasks. Perhaps you can hire someone to mow the lawn while you use that extra time to take your kids for ice cream. Or, if you can't afford to hire help, consider bartering. Because everyone's value scale will be different, it may just work out that you will find someone whose should-dos match up with your valued activities and vice versa. Also, don't forget delegation, which will be discussed in greater detail later in the chapter. It may simply be that you decide you can just forget about the task entirely. Perhaps it wasn't really that important in the first place and certainly isn't now in comparison to the valueds. If you can bring yourself to lower your standards for the should-dos, you can then raise your standards for the valueds.

Once you get rid of some of the should-dos, apply that time toward the valueds. Change the 20 percent to 40 percent. Only good can come from this, so why not make it work? All of a sudden, you will have an improved outlook on life, feel better about yourself and what you are doing, and be motivated to get more accomplished. Your ultimate goal is to spend more time on those activities that bring the most satisfaction. The 80/20 Rule may seem as though it is working against us, but really it helps us to keep our priorities in check. Come back to it once in a while and reevaluate your value system. You may find that the 80/20 Rule has snuck up on you once again.

Multitasking: Pros and Cons

What word comes to mind when you think of time management? Several people believe *multitasking* is the new, trendy word that holds the key to solving all time management problems. Multitasking is the idea that more than one task can be performed at once, thereby saving time. Sounds ideal, right? While there are several advantages to this concept, there are also disadvantages that many people don't take into consideration, or sometimes even choose to ignore. First, take a look at the advantages.

The Pros

Think about how often you waste time waiting—for the doctor, on hold, in lines, and in traffic. You spend most of those times grumbling to yourself, "I could be doing this or that." There is always something that could be done. For these situations, multitasking would work well. Here are some ways you can use it effectively:

- While waiting in the doctor's or dentist's office, finish off the last chapter of the novel you've been meaning to get to for the last few weeks. Not only will you be glad to finally find out who murdered Miss Smith, but you will have also successfully kept your mind off of the dreaded drill or shot.
- While watching television, you can accomplish several mindless, yet necessary, tasks. Fold the laundry, use your treadmill, clean, or iron.
- Multitasking while on the phone can be tricky sometimes. Because you are dealing with a person who expects your full attention, you can't do anything distracting. Wash dishes, unpack your groceries, or cook dinner. At work, straighten your desk or order office supplies. If you are talking with someone who has a tendency to dominate the conversation while saying a whole lot of nothing, however, then by all means get other things done. Just be fair to yourself and your caller—if the phone call is not more *important* than your other tasks, reschedule the call for another time.
- While waiting to pick up your kids from soccer practice, balance the checkbook.
- If you have a long commute to work, get the most from your car stereo. Listen to news radio and skip the paper; listen to foreign language instruction tapes or audiobooks. By stimulating your mind, you will be more alert while driving, as well as more energized once you reach your destination. Who knows, you might even be inclined to just smile at the guy who cut you off.
- Optimize your grocery shopping. Look through coupons and circulars, make your shopping list, and plan your menus all at once. The motivation behind this will be different for

everyone, so if you are a coupon clipper, plan your menu based on specials. If you're menu driven, start with the meals, compose the list, then see what's on sale. Regardless of your method, these are the benefits: you will accomplish two things in the space of one today; you will save money at the store tomorrow; and you will save time in the kitchen (or poring over take-out menus) all week.

- Open your mail, write personal notes, or shop online while eating lunch.

The Cons

Because of the technology that exists today, multitasking seems obligatory. Between pagers, Palm Pilots, voice mail, e-mail, and mobile phones, something is always ringing, beeping, or buzzing. Often, gizmos and gadgets do make completing tasks faster and easier. However, you must use these devices with sense and courtesy in the midst of the technology race. Take care when using them while driving, and turn off the ringer when an inter-ruption would be inappropriate. Use common sense—you have these tools to make your life easier, not to control you.

Multitasking works well with jobs that take little concentra-tion, but avoid it for jobs that require focus. Because you are working on two or more tasks at once, your attention will have to be divided. Poorly managed multitasking can actually cause you to lose time. If you don't devote your full attention to an impor-tant project, mistakes will occur, requiring you to take time to cor-rect your errors. However, if you concentrate solely on what you are trying to accomplish, chances are you will get the job done correctly and quickly the first time.

Some people feel guilty for not multitasking, which spurs them to acquire a collection of various partial tasks. The number of tasks completed is doubled, but the tasks themselves are often completed only half-sufficiently. So now, they can also feel guilty for not doing as well as they could. The pressure to overachieve has a significant impact on stress levels, which in turn can make them tired and careless.

In a world where multitasking gives you the image of success, it is easy to be lured into multitasking too often, even constantly. But be careful when succumbing to its appeal; your stress level and quality of work are at risk. The disadvantages of multitasking poorly will weigh heavily, but they can be overcome easily by using sound judgment. You will reap the greatest benefits if you save multitasking for jobs that require little focus and have minimal critical impact.

Quick Fix

Keep a realistic outlook. Bear in mind that it isn't how much you do, but how much you do well that marks you as a successful person.

The Costs of Multitasking

You pay in three important ways when you are compelled to juggle life's demands by doing several things at once. You lose focus, enthusiasm, and time.

The more hectic life becomes, the more the demands on your time mount, and the more you learn to do two, three, and four things at once, the less able you are to concentrate on what you're doing. The ability to become completely absorbed in an activity—so natural to children—becomes elusive; you can't recapture it even if you try.

When you lose your capacity for rapt attention, you also lose the childlike joy you once took from "being in the moment." Multitasking involves more than just the physical aspects of cradling a phone while you chop vegetables. It often involves watching your child's play, but thinking about your client presentation, making a mental to-do list, and wondering if you left the iron on. It's much harder to enjoy something if you aren't fully mentally invested in it.

Even if only half-appreciating where you are at any given moment doesn't bother you, the third price tag of multitasking should: the more you try to save time by doing more than one thing at once, the greater the risk of doing one, if not both, tasks wrong. Nothing takes longer, or is more frustrating, than having to redo your work. The ripple effect of a poorly done job will waste not only your time, but also the time of those who depend on you.

Distractions

How many times have you said, "I got distracted"? Probably thousands. It's one of the most prevalent excuses for missing a deadline, forgetting to pick up your kids, ruining dinner, or just about any blunder you can think of. As an excuse, it's widely accepted because everyone has to work around, or through, distractions.

A distraction is anything that pulls your attention away from what you are currently working on. Noise, the lack of noise, emergencies, television, a bird outside the window—these are all distractions. They are inevitable and have the potential to ruin your carefully planned schedules. There are, however, simple steps you can take to cut down on the damage.

A Welcome Distraction

First, realize that most distractions are a problem only because you allow them to be. In other words, the channel surfing in the other room may very well distract you to the point of insanity; whereas it may have no effect whatsoever on your partner. If you don't enjoy what you are doing, you may subconsciously search for a distraction. In this case, anything that diverts your attention is welcome although you may groan about it. But truly, you are finding a way to place the blame for your own lack of attention or involvement.

If you secretly welcome distractions, it may be that you simply have a lack of focus. This doesn't have to apply to everything you do. Perhaps you find yourself consistently distracted only when you are trying to write a paper or take notes in a meeting. That makes sense during activities you dislike. If you find that suddenly the color of the neighbor's grass becomes the most interesting thing you've ever noticed, take a look at what you should be working on. Staying focused on an irritating project is very difficult, but it can be done.

Control Distractions

You have control over some tangible distractions. For instance, if you are trying to write a paper, turn off the television so your eyes won't wander in that direction. Shut the door and blinds if necessary. Position your computer screen so there isn't a glare beckoning to you. Remove as many external distractions as you can. A controlled environment will help some, but if writing this paper is something you really dread, your own mind may turn against you.

Daydreaming is a favorite distraction. It doesn't need outside stimuli; instead it plays on your fantasies and lack of focus. Since you can't very well turn off your mind, you will need to find an alternate way of avoiding daydreams. In this case, you may want to use visual aids.

When you go into that "zone," it may seem as though you don't see things in front of you, but your eyes will still register them. Write a memo to yourself listing the reasons why this project is important to you, and place it within eyeshot. Or, if positive reinforcement doesn't work, make a list of the penalties you will have to pay if the project isn't completed.

Another suggestion is to let someone else know you are having trouble focusing. Ask that person to check up on you periodically to see how much you have accomplished. Chances are, you will feel a bit of pressure to get more done, and your focus will be a little more steady. Don't allow yourself to be checked on too frequently, though, because that will only serve as yet another distraction!

What Do Distractions Cost You?

Consider the amount of time distractions cost you. Do you often use distractions as your excuse for being late? If you stay focused on your project, it will be over quickly and out of your life. However, if you allow distractions to interfere continuously, it could drag the project out over a course of days. No one wants to wake up in the morning knowing they have to complete a dreaded task that could have been done the day before. That just gives you an even worse attitude toward the task, encouraging even more distractions. Try to focus on a positive aspect of the job, even if it is only getting it completed and out of the way.

Of course, there are distractions you can't avoid. Emergencies such as illness in the family, for example, cannot be anticipated. However, if you are a good time manager, you will have left some time available for the unexpected interruptions.

Keep in mind that distractions aren't always the enemy. If you have a tendency to become distracted quite frequently, this could be a warning sign. Some people become overwhelmed more frequently than others in this very busy age. Distracting ourselves may be a natural way of giving the mind some necessary downtime. Though it may seem like a contradiction, breaks are an important part of getting things accomplished. So pay attention to your inattention. You just may need to schedule a few more breaks to keep your mind clear.

Interruptions

One class of distraction is interruptions. An interruption is an interference in your schedule caused by an outside force. Most often people are the interruption, and that can sometimes be more difficult to deal with than a distraction. Though some people don't mind dissuading others from bothering them, other people find it difficult to discourage someone for fear of seeming insensitive, unfriendly, or downright rude. Regardless, interruptions must be dealt with if you want to strengthen your time management skills.

There are different degrees of interruption. Some you simply have to deal with. For example, a storm just blew a tree branch through your beautiful bay window. That's something that requires immediate attention. Luckily, the most common interruptions are ones that can be limited. It just takes a bit of skill and practice.

Got a Minute?

Socialization is necessary for comfort and happiness, right? But is it necessary at all times? Interruptions from people are a difficult thing to avoid. Yet, if you don't set some boundaries, your entire day can be consumed by nothing more than the ubiquitous "got a minute?" opening line. Because you are forced to deal with the interruption face to face, it is easy to give up your ground. Look for ways to dodge drawn-out interruptions without hurting the other's feelings or being labeled a recluse.

> **Hide.** It sounds like silly advice, but consider it extended body language. If you have a project to work on, find an area that is out of the high-traffic zone. People are more inclined to stop and chitchat if they see that you are "open." Instead, subtly conceal yourself by positioning your work area behind a partially closed door. You will still be available to people who really need your help,

but you can escape the wagging tongues of those who have nothing better to do. Unless they have something important to say, chances are people will respect your nonverbal cues, and keep on walking.

Make an announcement. Inform those around you that you have a lot of work to do and need to be left alone for a while. Stress the importance of the task if you feel that will help emphasize your point. Perhaps you could even ask them to take your phone calls or pick up the mail. Chances are, you'll clear the area if you start handing out assignments to all who stop to bother you.

Stand up when someone approaches you. This will make them less inclined to sit and stay a while. Also, maintain professional body language. Don't relax and neither will the interloper.

Always keep a bit of busywork close by. Even if it is a fake fax to be sent to your sister, keep it within reach. If you see a long-winded person approaching, grab the fax and offer to walk him down the hall. Don't let him get comfortable.

Look busy. This shouldn't be too difficult for you to do. Quite often people won't make you part of their rounds if you are visibly busy.

Set time limits. Let the visitor know how much time, if any, you have available. If things become too involved, ask if you can schedule a time to sit down and talk. This is a courteous way to plan for the discussion, and it also shows that you feel his concern is important enough to warrant an extended period of time.

Don't be afraid to shut the door. An open door is an invitation to many people.

Place a "Do Not Disturb" or "Quiet" sign outside your work area. If people don't take the hint after that, feel free to unleash the beast.

How to Delegate

If you feel as though you need to be everywhere at once in order to get things done, it may be time to stop what you are doing and delegate. For some, this can be a very scary idea. For others, it is a dream come true. Delegation is simply getting the job done by distributing the work. It is a relatively simple idea, but one that needs to be executed correctly if you want to save time and energy. Keep in mind that this isn't a power trip. Effective delegation is not barking orders; it is inviting someone to accept shared responsibility for the completion of a project.

Those who are serious about time management will learn to delegate. It will take some valuable time in the beginning, and that's a difficult commitment to make. It's time well spent, however, because the time you save in the long run more than makes up for it.

The most obvious advantage of delegating is that it means less busywork for you. In addition, those to whom you delegate will appreciate the trust you place in them, creating closer relationships. The work itself will become easier, and your stress level will decrease. Sometimes you will even find others who have the specialized skills to tackle a job with more efficiency and accuracy than you could.

When you hear "delegate," you probably think of workplace responsibilities. However, if you apply the concept to work you do with your friends and family (don't forget the children!), delegation can improve most areas of your life. Time management isn't necessarily restricted to just work, so why should the tools that help you manage it be?

Quick Fix

It's good for your time management system if you delegate tasks, but don't take it too far. Remember: Others are trying to manage their time effectively as well.

The Delegation Process

In order to make delegation work for you instead of against you, consider the following suggestions. As with the many new skills you're learning, learning to be comfortable delegating will take time and practice. If you rush through it, you may be costing yourself more in the long run.

> **Make a decision.** Before you start passing out assignments, you must decide what needs to be delegated. Create a prioritized list of jobs that have yet to be completed. Spend a bit of time with each item and consider whether there is someone who has the skills necessary to finish it for you. Take into consideration which jobs bring you the greatest gain. Your focus should remain with these, whereas jobs that yield a lower return are prime candidates for delegation. When you first begin to delegate, you may keep the most critical jobs under your control. By delegating less important tasks first, you will adjust to trusting others, and others will get used to you.
>
> **Choose with care.** Choosing the right person for the job is a major part of the process. Matching a person's skills to the job should be foremost in your mind. However, also respect others' wishes. A person who doesn't currently have the skills to tackle a task successfully, may be eager learn them. Delegated jobs provide excellent training—you are supervising just enough to stay involved in the project, and your motivated protégé may be more committed than someone who has done this a hundred times already. Just be sure you have enough time to do the supervising.
>
> **Give specific instructions.** Once you have decided who is going to get what job, be very clear in your expectations. Explain exactly what needs to be done, why it needs to

be done, and when it should be done. Provide training, if necessary, but don't hold an employee's hand. Giving a person the authority to make some decisions and complete a job will give him the confidence and assurance he needs to prove himself. Also keep in mind that working on an entire project is more satisfying (and instructive) than working on just bits and pieces.

Trust the person to get it done. Do not stand over her shoulder, watching her every move. The idea behind delegation is to create more time for yourself. Not only will you waste your time by worrying and constantly checking up on the project, but you will also jeopardize the trusting relationship you're trying to establish. Tension and nervousness in the person trying to do the work will raise the potential for mistakes.

Communicate effectively. You must keep the lines of communication open. Let the worker know you are available to answer questions, but encourage him to try his own ideas first. This will not only show that you support his work, but it will give him confidence in his own judgment as well. Prearrange meetings to review the project status. A casual yet organized forum is an unobtrusive way for you to supervise without hovering, and for him to ask questions without continually interrupting his work, or yours.

Allow for mistakes—they are good learning tools. If you have done a good job delegating, the little mistakes will be easy to fix.

Above all, praise the person for a job well done.

Delegation Hang-Ups

Even though delegation sounds like an easy fix, some people would still rather take everything on themselves. The reasons for this vary from person to person, and all are reasonable. If you identify with the following characteristics, however, work to overcome them. You won't be able to delegate effectively, or manage your time efficiently, until you do.

Some people like to think they are superhuman and want to maintain that image. Yet these are the same people who find themselves constantly taking on more than they can possibly handle. If they are able to accomplish everything they've committed to, it is unlikely that the tasks are done well. The probable result is self-induced stress, faulty projects, and one tired and grumpy soul.

Perhaps you suffer from perfectionism or aren't willing to give control of a project to someone else. The very thought of allowing others to take over your tasks, and possibly do them "wrong," makes you cringe. You like things to be done perfectly (or your way) and rarely trust anyone else to do that kind of work. You are probably the person most in need of delegating skills. If this description seems to fit you, you are most likely at your wit's end trying to get everything done and done well. But sometimes it just isn't possible. Learn to divvy up the work. It is better to get a project completed with a few mistakes than not started at all.

Another common hang-up is that you just don't have the time to sacrifice. This is a pretty good argument, considering you are already having problems managing your time. But one of the fundamentals of time management is prioritizing and looking ahead. Delegating, if you plan on doing it right, will undoubtedly take time in the beginning. But remember that it will save you immeasurable time in the long run. You may not see the results right away, but eventually they will show. If you live in the "now," this will probably serve only to frustrate you. But if you are concerned with your future, delegation is a smart route to take.

chapter four

You Set the Agenda

Working Effectively with Others

You already know that when it comes to scheduling, you should expect the unexpected. Your day planner is bursting with to-do lists, deadlines, and commitments. And so is everyone else's.

Just as you may rely heavily on others for information, input, or attendance, they will rely on you. Whether it's a report you need to provide, or a last-minute request to attend a meeting or event, you will be called upon to deliver something you haven't worked into your schedule.

The problem arises when you're so bogged down with what you need—or want—to do that you don't have time for impromptu calls or visits. Learn how to manage not only your time, but also the people who make unexpected demands on it.

Just Three Little Words

The phone rings. You snatch it up before it can ring again.

"Are you busy?" the voice on the other end asks.

Or "Got a minute?"

A flippant response ("For you?") can be so tempting. But you're a conscientious and caring human being. You've learned that the customer is always right and that everybody, including each of your colleagues, is, in one way or another, your customer. So, instead of sarcasm or confrontation, you probably reply with something along the lines of, "Now's fine," or "Fire away," or "How may I help you?"

You've just signed a blank check, and the caller gets to fill in the amount. Those three little words—"Got a minute?"—may be stealing your life, a few minutes at a time. You can stop this time erosion, and you can probably do it without hurting anybody's feelings.

Take it from the top, from the moment somebody asks "Got a minute?" and see if you can work out a response someplace between "Why, sure. Take all you want" and "Buzz off."

What's Wrong with "Buzz Off"?

An inappropriate (whether it's mildly unhelpful or downright rude) response won't win you many friends—or customers—or influence people, either. Beyond that, you may want and need to have the conversation being offered to you. You have the right and obligation to decide.

You get to decide how you spend your time, which is to say that you get to decide what you'll do right now, this minute.

To make a smart decision about the "Got a minute?" telephone question, you need two critical pieces of information:

1. What does the caller want to talk about?
2. How much time does the caller want?

When you have this information, you can decide *if* you'll talk and, if so, for how long.

You have the right to ask. In fact, you're not managing your time well if you don't.

Be Nice

"How may I help you?" is a good place to start, since it focuses on the needs of the caller while eliciting the information you need. You can no doubt come up with several more ways to determine if you do need to attend to a request immediately. If you think it will be helpful, write your questions down. Keep them by the phone as a reminder and cue card until you feel comfortable asking.

What about that old standby, "No"? Is it ever OK to answer "Got a minute?" with a simple "No"? Of course. You get to decide, remember? If you really don't have a minute, "No" is the right as well as the accurate response.

You can follow it up by buying a little time ("Can I get back to you in about half an hour?") or by setting a specific time to talk. That way, you've asserted control over the situation and your schedule. Note, though, that you've still signed a blank check; you've just postdated it. You still don't know what the conversation is going to be about, and you still don't know if you really want or need to have the conversation at all.

Find a Way Out

If you're struggling with ways of buying yourself time, or getting your caller to get straight to the point, consider the following ways of handling calls and other interruptions.

- "I don't have time to talk. I'm really busy right now."
- "Can we catch up on all of this over lunch?"
- "If you don't have anything to do, can you run some of these errands for me?"

- "Now is really not a good time for me."
- "I'm in the middle of something, but please send me an e-mail and let me know when you need the information."
- "Will you excuse me? I need to make an important phone call."
- "I'm sorry, you'll have to schedule an appointment with my assistant."

The Golden Rule

If you practice an effective response to "Got a minute?" long enough, you'll train some of your frequent interrupters to ask the right question in the first place, a question that will supply the information you need in order to determine if this is the best time for you. "I need about five minutes to discuss the Aarons project with you. Is this a good time?"

Don't forget to think about your own approach. Is that the way you open a conversation, or are you just as guilty of the "Got a minute?" question as everyone else? Get in the practice of asking others as you would like them to ask you.

Quick Fix

Whether you're leaving a message, sending an e-mail, or talking directly to someone, state the purpose of your inquiry. Others will have enough information to decide whether they can provide more effective help now or later.

Why Nice Guys Finish Last

Your urge to be overly accommodating may have its roots in weakness, not strength. Eventually, you will have to find a way to be helpful and effective without being a doormat. In the meantime, consider whether any (or many) of the following sound familiar.

1. **Looking for love in all the right causes.** You earn the gratitude and approval of your peers when you shoulder their burdens. The anticipation of approval and acceptance may, in part, fuel your need to say yes. Behind this desire may even lurk the fear that, if you don't work so hard, those around you will stop accepting you.

2. **The guilt syndrome.** "It's difficult to say 'no' when someone asks you to serve on a not-for-profit board, chair a committee, or attend a fund-raiser for a very worthy cause," writes Jan Benson Wright, editor of *The Peoria Woman*. "When we decline, we are often inclined to shoulder a subsequent burden of guilt, because 'superwoman' failed to come through as expected."

3. **The myth of indispensability.** Arrogance, rather than kindness, may, in part, motivate your efforts. Perhaps you don't let others do the job because, deep down, you don't believe anyone else can do it, or do it as well as you can. You've taken to heart the adage, "If you want a job done right, do it yourself."

4. **The fear of expendability.** What if you didn't show up for work and nobody noticed? On some basic, subconscious level, you may be afraid that the moment you stop all of your efforts, people will discover that they don't really need you at all.

Reasons three and four seem mutually exclusive. They're not. It's quite possible to feel both ways at the same time. Just as you can be in a "love/hate relationship," you can feel both indispensable and expendable.

If, like most people, you see yourself in the prior profiles, think about what motivates your behavior. There is nothing wrong with being accommodating, in and of itself. The problems lie in the undue stress and responsibilities you bring on yourself. It's fulfilling to help people, be knowledgeable, and know that you are an expert. That fulfillment, however, may be overshadowed by resentment and frustration, which will affect your overall performance

Manage Meeting Black Holes

Somewhere during the middle of the 1980s, folks stopped merely talking to each other. Whenever two or more people gather in the workplace, it's become a "meeting." People don't even just meet anymore. They "have a meeting" or "take a meeting." Raise the level of rhetoric and you raise the apparent value. "We need to have a meeting" somehow sounds much more important than "Got a minute?"

But whether it's a summit conference or a casual chat, you still have the same basic right to decide whether you want to have, or take, or do it.

Many have itchy fingers when it comes to calendars and day planners. You hear the word "meeting" and whip out the schedules.

—*"How about next Tuesday?"*
—*"No good. I'm on the road."*
—*"Wednesday?"*
—*"What time?"*
—*"2:00?"*
—*"No good. I've got the Benson meeting."*
—*"How long will that take?"*
—*"At least until 4:00."*

—*"How about then?"*

—*"No, I have to be in Milwaukee by 5:00."*

So it goes, until someone finds a common hole in the wall of appointments, often extending the workday to do it.

—*"OK. We'll meet at the donut shop at 4:00 A.M."*

Before you wind up with crumbs on your shirt at four in the morning, assert your right to ask questions and decide based on the answers you get, before you commit. You need to know:

1. What's the subject matter?
2. Does it really require a meeting? (Maybe you can talk about it for two minutes right now and avoid having to meet later.)
3. Are you the person to do the talking, now or later?

Recovering from Phone Addiction

Everyone has benefited from technology, but do you ever find yourself just wanting to rip the phone right out of the wall? Few can deny the urgency of the ringing apparatus, right within an arm's reach.

Phone calls are an acceptable distraction because it isn't your fault someone called. Besides, phone calls don't last very long, and it may be an emergency. Track your phone usage for a couple of days. Mark down who called, for what reason, how long the call lasted, and then rate its importance. You can do this for a couple of weeks and become thoroughly shocked, but just a couple of days should open your eyes.

Phone Usage

Name of Caller	Reason for Call	Time Spent	Importance
Doug	Scheduling visit	15 minutes	7
Michelle	Department meeting	10 minutes	5
Mom	Just to talk	10 minutes	9
Randy	Sales meeting	20 minutes	8
Doctor Smith	Blood work	5 minutes	3
Alicia	Marketing proposal	25 minutes	4
Larry	Status of Martin proposal	20 minutes	1
Tara	Client queries	15 minutes	2
Brian	Stocks	5 minutes	6

If you find that your phone calls total more time than you spend actually working, it's definitely time to limit yourself. Here are some suggestions to help you get started on the phone addict's road to recovery:

Shut off your ringer and let the voice mail or answering machine pick it up. If you don't know it's ringing, you won't feel the compulsion to answer. Even if you do it only while you are completing a project, the time you save will amaze you. Not only are you saving the time it takes to carry out the conversation, but also the period of time it takes to get focused again on your project.

Use Caller ID. If you just can't bring yourself to shut off the ringer (or perhaps knowing that the phone's not ringing would be a major distraction in itself), install an identification feature that will allow you to see who is calling before you decide whether to answer it. Screening your calls won't lower the number of interruptions, but it will reduce the overall amount of time spent on interruptions. This will work only if you refrain from answering every call.

Designate a period of time in your day to return and make phone calls. For optimum payoff, schedule this time to coincide with your least productive time of day. Making phone calls doesn't necessarily take a lot of energy or attention and could serve as a break from a project. Also, let others know that this is the best time to reach you. If they call in the time slot already allowed for phone calls, that cuts back on the number of unexpected interruptions in the day.

Get right to the point. It isn't necessary to find out how each member of the family is doing or what the weather is like in Cleveland. On the other hand, be pleasant. Begin by asking what it is you can do for the person. This will encourage the caller to get right to the point without participating in idle chatter.

Set time limits. You can politely set limits by immediately informing the caller that you have only a few moments to spare. Not only will the caller be aware of, and try to keep within, the time limit, but also he may feel honored that you chose to spend your valuable time speaking with him.

Don't humor a salesperson just to be polite. Some people feel it is rude to deny a salesperson or telemarketer her right to talk. But think about it: The motive behind the call is to make a sale. If you aren't interested, say so right away. Otherwise, the salesperson will waste your time and hers by reciting her entire speech just to have you decline the offer anyway. Do not tell her to send you the information in the mail unless you're truly interested in the offer. Otherwise, you will waste time when she verifies your mailing address, in addition to almost guaranteeing another phone call within a couple of weeks and more sorting of snail mail.

Don't Be Bullied

No amount of figuring, calculating, or deciding will do you a bit of good if you aren't able to act on your decisions. Know yourself, and know your motivations. Then, consider any number of requests that come your way, and your possible answers.

1. **Beware the automatic yes.** You may have gotten into your time trouble because you have a very hard time saying no. But you've learned through bitter experience that it's much harder to get out of something later than to turn it down now.

2. **Buy time.** Unless you're already certain of your response one way or the other, ask for time to think about it. This is both a reasonable and a truthful response that allows you to make an informed and considerate decision. You really do want and need time to think about it.

3a. **If the answer is no, say no.** Say it gracefully, but say it.

3b. **You don't have to give a reason.** This may come as a shock: People are reasonable. They are motivated by reason, and want others to understand and agree with their rationale for their decisions. They want people to continue to think well of them, and give reasons. Unfortunately, that opens the issue to discussion. More often than not, the persuasion debate is a losing battle. The negative position is a much harder stance to support.

When making a decision, use your informed understanding of your motives and the true costs and benefits of the activity. Then stick to your decision. You'll find yourself with a more conscious control of your life, and that control will buy you a lot more time to do what you want and need to be doing.

chapter five

Time Management for Managers

Tips for Dealing with Staff

Managing people takes time. It may take an inefficient or ineffective manager longer to plan, supervise, and evaluate someone else's work than to just do it himself. The answer is *not* to fire the staff. The answer is to manage them effectively. Here are seven time management tips that will help you do it.

1. **Never waste their time.** Does the sight of one of your workers standing idle threaten you? If so, resist the temptation to assign busywork just to keep them moving. You waste their time, of course, and you also waste your time thinking up the work, explaining and supervising it, and pretending to care about it when it's done.

   You'll also be eroding their trust in you and your decisions. They'll know it's busywork!

Don't fill their time for them. Show them what needs doing. Show them how to do it. Make sure they have the tools they need. Then get out of the way.

2. **Make sure time savers are really saving time.** The fax is supposed to save time, right? But people soon learn to fax letters that could have (should have?) gone by good old pony express, and put off writing the letter until it has to go by fax. That doesn't save time; it just increases pressure.

There's no reason to retreat to the Stone Age. Few would consider trying to write without a computer, research without the Internet, or handle phone calls without voice mail. But these good slaves can make terrible masters, and can drive your staff to distraction with bells, beeps, and buzzers. Make sure the machines work for the people and not the other way around.

3. **Separate the important from the merely urgent for your staff.** For your staff, as for yourself, you need to distinguish between truly important activities, those that serve the central mission, and the stuff that seems to demand immediate attention when they don't really merit any attention at all.

Do you and your staff ever engage in long-term planning, skills training, or career development, or do these things get lost in the daily clamor? You'll never "find" time to do these important (but seldom urgent) activities with your staff. As a good manager, you must be sure to make the time.

Ask "Why?" for the phone calls and memos and faxes demanding your staff's immediate attention. Can you relieve some of the pressure and release your staffers to more important work?

4. **Give them reasons.** "How come I have to do this?" If that question from a staffer feels like a threat to your

authority, or if you become defensive when you hear such a question, your staffers will learn to keep the questions to themselves. But they'll still wonder.

They have the right and the need to know the purpose behind your assignment. When you ask them to do something, also give them the reason. You'll have a more motivated and more efficient workforce, with a better understanding of you and their role in the big picture.

5. **Allow enough time for the task.** Be realistic in your demands, and don't overstress the staff. If you do, you'll get shoddy work. You might even get less work. Even a conscientious, willing worker doesn't perform well under unreasonable pressure.

6. **Encourage your staff to do one thing at a time and do it well.** Watch your staff at work. Are they on the phone, jotting notes, eyeing the computer screen, all while trying to grab a fast sandwich? Maybe.

Are they getting a lot done? Probably not. And they're probably not getting anything done well.

If your coworker is on the phone with a potential client, you want that worker's total attention on the task at hand, not thinking about the next project or the last project or the work that isn't getting done. Employees concentrating on one thing at a time work faster and better, with less need for clarification or revision.

7. **Cut down on meeting time!** If you asked your staff to list "urgent but not important" and "neither urgent nor important" activities in the workplace, chances are "go to a meeting" will appear on most lists. Most people hate meetings. They avoid them if they can; resent them when they can't; and complain about them before, during, and after. So, the first tip here ought to be obvious: Don't have a meeting if you don't have a good reason to meet.

Does that mean eliminate all meetings? Of course not. You really do need meetings in order to create a productive interaction that can't happen with a memo, e-mail, phone call, or one-on-one conversation. People get a better grasp of the whole operation when they see all the critical players. Names become faces, and faces become individuals. You can develop and maintain a sense of shared purpose and cooperation. In a meeting:

- Everyone hears the same thing at the same time, removing some (but not all) miscommunication.
- Attendees have an opportunity to ask for clarification if they have any questions.
- The speaker can note nonverbal clues (crossed arms, frowns, glazed eyes, eager nodding) to determine how people are responding.
- Most important, when people interact, they create ideas that never would have occurred otherwise.

Cutting Unproductive Meetings

Schedule regular meetings. If you don't have a reason to meet, or if you have reasons not to meet, you can always cancel. Nobody ever complains about a canceled meeting.

Every time you do have a meeting, make it worth your staff's time and energy to be there. Here's how.

Before the Meeting

1. **Be prepared.** You really have to know your stuff to explain it to others. Do your homework. Review your reason(s) for holding the meeting and the outcome(s) you want.

2. **Get the meeting place ready.** Make sure the flip chart and markers and overhead projector are in place (and working!). How about visuals? Refreshments? Seating arrangements? Put the chairs in rows facing front if you want people to sit quietly and listen passively. Arrange seating around a table if you expect attendees to take an active part in the discussion.

3. **Get others prepared.** Don't pass out copies of a thick report to start the meeting and then expect folks to read and react on the spot. Even the most willing worker won't be able to do a good job.

   What do they need to know before the meeting? Get information to them at least two working days ahead of time. Some won't read it, but many will, and they'll come prepared.

4. **Set and communicate an agenda.** Whatever else you send them before the meeting, be sure to circulate an agenda. Emphasize action items and spell out recommendations you plan to make. If people need to bring something with them (like their calendars so you can plan yet another meeting), tell them now.

   Be sure to include the day, place, and time for the meeting.

During the Meeting

5. **Keep it focused and positive.** Don't let your meeting degenerate into personal attack or disintegrate into multiple sidebar discussions.

Here are a few ground rules you may find helpful:

- Use "I" statements in sharing your perceptions.

Not: "This meeting is a stupid waste of time."

But: "I feel like we're wasting our time here."

- Talk about issues, not personalities.

Not: "Your idea is idiotic."

But: "I don't think this idea will work because . . . "

- Listen actively. Don't interrupt.
- Don't yell, pound the table, or curse.

Although these ideas are not new, revisit them occasionally. If your situation requires special considerations, develop guidelines or ground rules that work for your group.

Don't Waste Time with Indecision

If you're responsible for managing time—your own or someone else's—you have to be clear in your direction. You may have a lot of good ideas, but if you can't choose one and act on it, your team will suffer. Your failure to make decisions will affect productivity and morale.

Indecision may be costing you in ways you haven't even thought of. When you delay making a decision, you also delay taking action based on that decision. You spend additional time weighing the pros and cons, you lose focus on the task at hand, and you squander precious energy worrying and second-guessing yourself.

You may be paying in terms of how others view you, too. If you're chronically slow to reach a decision, the people you work with may learn to place little trust in you. Although you might think of yourself as thoughtful and deliberate, they may see you as indecisive at best, or worse, weak and incapable.

It works the other way, too, of course. When you think of yourself as decisive and resolute, others may view you as inflexible or unwilling to see the merits in others' ideas.

"To be or not to be. That is the question."

Thus begins one of the most famous soliloquies in all of literature. Fortunately for *Hamlet,* which needed five acts, the young prince couldn't decide on anything. Brilliantly indecisive, he could see the wisdom in both sides of any argument, but he couldn't take any course of action.

If you can't decide whether or not to act, inaction wins by default. Your everyday conflicts need and deserve a firm decision, not a decision by default. Even though many conflicts require that you first generate a variety of potential options, as long as you fail to, or refuse to, decide, nothing gets done.

Three Fears

What makes a person indecisive? One or more of these common pitfalls could be getting in your way:

1. The fear of uncertainty
2. The fear of ignorance
3. The fear of error

You Don't Have to Be Certain to Be Sure

"Are you sure?" Three seemingly innocent little words can cripple your will.

Others may appear to you to be more confident in their decision making than you feel yourself. They aren't, you know. You see only their actions. You're not around when worry keeps them awake at night, and you can't see the doubt underneath their actions.

Your acute awareness of your own uncertainties and fears may lead you to believe that others are more decisive than you'll ever be. It's an illusion. Most people have doubts, and every reasonably intelligent human being can see at least two sides to every question. The difference is that some people are much more willing to act. The doers have "the strength of their convictions," regardless of how strong those convictions really are.

How certain do you have to be before you act? You don't have to be certain at all. You just have to be sure. Sure can be as little as 50.1 percent certain (about the margin that elected John F. Kennedy president).

Quick Fix

Make your best judgment and act on it. Frontiersman Davy Crockett said it best: "Be sure you're right, then go ahead."

You Can Never Know Enough

"If only I had known." Dwelling on hindsight will stall you every time.

Occasionally, the information and insight necessary to make a *fully* informed decision comes too late to use it. The result can be frustrating and even enraging, as when you lay out a lot of money for a major purchase, then find out you could have gotten it for considerably less elsewhere. It can also be embarrassing if someone finds out about your costly gaff or if you yourself feel that you should have known better.

The anger and embarrassment can be helpful if they prompt you to act more wisely next time, by comparison shopping before you buy, for example. It's always good to learn from a mistake so that you don't make the same mistake again. But those negative feelings can work against you if they render you unwilling or unable to act the next time you face a major decision. Your fear of looking or feeling like a chump can paralyze you.

If you insist on gathering all the information and anticipating all the potential outcomes before you make a decision, you'll never act. Be comfortable with the fact that you don't need to know it all.

Let hindsight teach you so you can make better and better decisions, but leave the second-guessing to the critics. You don't have time for such nonsense.

A "Wrong" Decision Is Better Than No Decision

"Play to win," coaches say, meaning, don't play just to avoid losing, or you'll be stiff and cautious. But most people are trained to do just the opposite.

> There you are in the "Magpie" reading group, working out Dick's and Jane's relationships with Mom and Dad, Spot and Puff. You make a mistake, everybody laughs, and you feel like a fool. Teacher corrects you, and you stumble on, trying not to step on the next land mine.
>
> You do your best on that essay about your summer vacation, and it comes back with the misspellings circled and the sentence fragments tagged.
>
> The only marks on that math exam are the slashes through the wrong answers.

Unfortunately, this perspective often carries over into the world of work, where too often the only feedback you get is negative.

To steal another line from Hamlet, nothing but negative feedback tends to "make cowards of us all." Instead of accepting the risk—and the opportunity to learn that comes with it—that comes from making a decision, you fear the fallout of taking a chance. Wasting time postponing and fussing over decisions because you're afraid of making mistakes comes at the price of action and progress.

"Haste makes waste," but that isn't necessarily a bad thing. You can clean up the waste. Because when it comes right down to it, especially in business, "He who hesitates is lost." Convinced that you're better off deciding than not deciding? Good. Now do it quickly and effectively.

Seven Tips for Making Decisions

As with most things, balance is critical to effectively make decisions. Look for balance between haste and immobility. Know enough to make an educated guess, but be comfortable with the uncertainty that comes from taking a risk. The following tips are generalizations, certainly, but will keep you grounded—and confident in yourself.

1. **Stay open to the "third side."** Most issues have three or four (or five) sides, approaches, or ways of looking at them. You don't want to ponder possibilities forever, but you do need to get as many options as possible on the table within a limited time frame. That way, you won't keep stumbling over options that make you postpone your decision, nor will you doubt the decisions you've already made.

2. **Cast your nets widely.** Sometimes you can't make a decision because you just don't know enough yet. You need to consult the experts—and you need to be open about how you define *expert*. Your best source of information may carry a fancy title and a big reputation, or he or she may answer the phones or work on the line. The ones closest to the problems often have the insights you need to solve them.

   Don't hesitate to seek input from anyone who can help you make a swift decision.

3. **Consider the consequences.** Lay out potential actions side by side on a sheet of paper or flip chart (or visual medium of choice). Make note of the pros and cons out where you can see them; chart out the cause and effects of each option. Using words to compare possible outcomes with your ultimate goal will help you clarify your thinking. With any luck, by the time you

finish your list, your solution may present itself.

4. **Count the pot.** Be sure you know what's at stake. Do an informal cost or risk analysis. What's the worst that can happen? What are the odds of it happening? Decide whether the gains outweigh the risks.

5. **Talk it through.** Writing down your thoughts helps you clarify them. So does trying to explain them to somebody else; not only will you hear things differently, but you'll also get the added benefit of feedback from a different perspective. Talk out your dilemma to someone willing to listen and able to help.

6. **Sleep on it.** The goal is to speed up the process, but if possible, do your homework early enough for you to delay the decision overnight—or over lunch, or over a walk down the hall and back, if that's all the time you can give it. A little time away from the conscious tussle gives your subconscious a chance to play with ideas. You should come back to the issue clear-headed, refreshed, and maybe with a new idea that incorporates the best of your other options.

   Even in the heat of the most pressure-packed decision making, you can usually buy a little time if you need to. "Let me call you back in five minutes" can give you a chance to collect the thoughts and words you need to make the decision and to express it clearly.

7. **Just do something.** Get input. Make your list. Then make the call and get on with it.

Sell the Call!

Do you want to find an expert on making decisions? Talk to the folks with the whistles, striped shirts, or blue coats who have to make split-second calls in the midst of huge, adrenaline-charged athletes, while countless critics are watching. If you want to find a decision maker, talk to an umpire or referee.

Sports officials are practiced experts when it comes to preparation, knowing the rules, being in position to make the call, and hustling even harder than the players do. They also know the one thing that makes them truly effective: You can't just make the decision; you have to sell it. Make your "safe" or "out" clear and emphatic so that folks understand the call and your authority to make it.

Does that mean you'll never make a mistake? Of course not. You won't make any fewer than anyone else—nor will making decisions rapidly and emphatically necessarily increase the number of errors you do make.

What to Do When You Blow the Call

Mistakes happen. Any customer-service provider will tell you that the key to good service is not the absence of error, but the speed and success with which an error is resolved. Keep that in mind with your own mistakes.

1. Admit it.
2. Make it right.
3. Get on with it.

Take your lumps. The people who work with you already know you're human. They just want to be sure you know it, too. Do whatever you can to right the wrong, which includes apologizing, if necessary. Then get back to work.

Eliminating Mistakes

No one errs on purpose, and some mistakes can have negative consequences. As a good manager, however, you don't worry about who is to blame when your team makes a mistake. Don't dwell on it for yourself either. There is a lesson in every mistake, even if it's only what not to do next time. Make the effort to find the meaning in yours.

When you start noting the pattern to your errors, you can start anticipating and eliminating them.

Quick Fix

You may want to focus attention on your errors in a more formal way. Create a checklist for troubleshooting your own performance, either before or after the fact. You'll notice whether you consistently make the same mistakes, and will know what to look for in the future. Keep the list as a living document, eliminating some items as you master them and adding others as they occur.

chapter six

Taming the Paper Tiger

Control the Paper Avalanche

"I'm a paper pusher." Shocking, but true. Your intentions were to be effective and impactive—and you probably are—but your overwhelming feeling is that, well, you're a paper pusher.

You spend from 50 to 70 percent of your working time dealing with paper—writing it, reading it, filing it, or, most likely, looking through it for something else. If you're ever going to get control of your time—which is to say your life—you're going to have to control the paper flood.

Control, Reduce, and Eliminate Paper

Adopt a constant companion. Keep a bound notebook with you all the time—in your attaché case, in your desk drawer, in your coat pocket or purse, on your night table. Capture stray insights and write yourself reminders. This way you won't lose your ideas because they'll be in one place, and you won't wind up with scraps of paper cluttering your life.

Manage your desktop(s). "A place for everything and everything in its place." That goes for your desktops both tangible and virtual.

It isn't a matter of being neat, it's about getting organized. Your desktop may extend to the floor and every other flat capable of holding piles and files. As long as you know where everything is and can lay your hands on it without having to wade through the stuff you don't want, you're in good shape. If others can follow your system, however, you'll be in better shape.

Touch it once. The first time you handle print—from a single-page memo to a 500-page report—decide what to do with it. Then do it. You can:

- Reroute
- Respond
- Read
- Recycle

Exercise good *sortsmanship*. Start by asking a variation of that fundamental question you developed a few chapters back: Do you want or need to deal with it? If not, does anybody need to? If so, reroute. If not, recycle.

Do it now. Keep a supply of routing slips, interoffice mail envelopes, and whatever else you need to send the stuff on its way right away. And keep a bucket for recycling within easy reach.

For anything that makes it past this first cut, create a simple system for categorizing every piece of paper you encounter. You don't need anything fancy here. File folders will do fine. You may need no more than three files: DO, READ, and FILE.

Make it disappear. There's only one thing better than getting rid of a document as soon as you touch it, and that's never having to touch it at all.

Never automatically renew a subscription without balancing the periodical's worth to you with the time it takes to process it. Ask to be taken off mailing lists and routing slips. For a wholesale purge of third-class mail, write to the Direct Marketing Association, Mail Reference Service, Box 3861, New York, NY 10163-3861, and get off all those lists!

RSVP ASAP. If the paper needs only a brief response, do it right now. Create a speed response:

- A personalized Post-it note
- A note written on the bottom of the original letter or memo
- A half-sheet of business letterhead for a short note
- A phone call if that is appropriate and more efficient

Are you being callous by sending the correspondent's own paper back to him or her? Not at all. Callous is putting off the response or not responding at all. You're being responsive and smart, and you're also saving paper.

File it and forget it? Do you really need to keep this document for your records?

Most people never refer back to, or even read, three-quarters of the stuff they file. Why take the time to file it now and to stumble over it haphazardly in the future? Practice source-point pollution control.

If you do need to hang on to the paper, put it in the appropriate filing folder. Schedule a short filing session once a day (or week or month, depending on the volume of paper you're dealing with) for a time when you're not at your mental peak.

Strip, clip, and flip. Tear out the material you really need and toss the rest of the publication. Be especially attentive to lists, tabulations, charts, and graphs that summarize a great deal of material in a small space. Recycle the rest.

While you're at it, throw away periodicals more than a year old, earlier drafts of written material, and old reports that no longer have relevance. Schedule a brief session at the end of each week so the clutter level never gets unmanageable. While you're engaged in relatively mindless work, you can decompress from a hard week of work, ease your transition into evening and weekend leisure time, and reflect on lessons learned.

Shift gears when you read. Reading everything at the same rate and in the same way makes as much sense as driving at the same speed on all roads and under all conditions.

Skim some materials for main ideas, scan others for specific information, and speed-read still others for their general tone. Save the material that requires time and concentration for your peak energy times, and for times when you can concentrate without interruption. Reading difficult material requires your best effort, not the last shreds of consciousness at the end of the day.

The cop-out compost heap. If you can adhere to the "touch it once" rule at all times, you'll save yourself tons of time. You'll also qualify for the Time Management Hall of Fame. If, however, that rule's a little too rigid, create another file category: the compost heap.

Can't decide what to do with it? Not sure you should do anything at all? Put it in the compost file and forget it. Once a week, get out the pitchfork and turn that compost. Some of the stuff will have more relevance for you now, so you'll want to deal with it right away. You'll also find that the majority of the documents is obsolete, and is now ready to go directly into the recycle bin.

Paper management will become a happy habit that will not only save you time and energy, but will also eliminate physical and mental clutter. All in all, it will reduce both stress and frustration from your workday and work space.

Quick Fix

Set aside time each week to review papers in the to-be-filed folder. You'll clear clutter in your work space, eliminate unnecessary paperwork, and keep your files under control.

Clutter Control

Sadly, the majority of people who lose weight on diets gain all the weight back—often with interest. While on the diet, they may totally change their eating habits. Often, however, the change in habits is only temporary. If you go back to old behavior patterns when you attain your target weight, the weight will inevitably sneak back.

The same rules apply to work space clutter. Ridding yourself of useless piles and files is one thing; keeping them at bay is quite another.

You'll still need to devote a set amount of time each day to maintain your clutter-free space. You might not need five minutes out of every hour, like before; it could be more like fifteen minutes at the end of the day—whether it's emptying your inbox before you leave the office for the day or clearing your mail off the kitchen table before you go to bed.

Incoming!

As you learned earlier, paper management isn't only taming the tiger you've created. You also need to apply effective and efficient techniques to the incoming paper flow.

Schedule a time each workday to deal with the incoming mail and memos. Be prepared with waste and recycle baskets, calendar, address book, file folders, Post-its, and stick-on dots. Now you're ready for a six-step process to reduce, control, and eliminate.

1. **Toss envelopes immediately.** Most addresses worth keeping are either at the top of a letter or in the letterhead itself. If that is not the case, as with cards or referrals, clip the return address from the envelope and slip it into your address book, or clip it onto the report.

2. **Note meeting and other appointment times on your calendar.** Then, unless you need the paper for some other reason, get rid of it.

3. **Create the file now.** If you need to save a document (are you sure?) and don't already have a place for it (are you sure of that, too?), create the file for it now, mark it carefully, and put it away.

4. **Schedule it.** If the material is going to require a longer and more thoughtful response, jot yourself a quick note on either the document or a Post-it indicating what you want to say and do, and when you plan on doing it.

Don't toss the note or the paper in your "to-do later" file until you've also marked your schedule with the corresponding information.

5. **Prune the periodicals.** You may be on the routing list for a lot of periodicals you don't really need to read. But even handling that newsletter, deciding not to read it, and sending it along to the next name on the list require time. Get yourself off those routing lists.

   In cases where you do need to review the periodical or communication, learn to skim it. If you find something you want to read, clip it from the periodical if it's yours, or make a photocopy if it isn't. Get rid of the remainder. Put your clips and copies in a "current reading" folder for your reading time, whether it's how you pass time on the subway, or fill the time you spend waiting in an airport or reception area.

6. **Affix the deadly red dot.** It doesn't have to be a red dot, really—any color will do. But whatever color you pick, mark everything you can't file, toss, recycle, or turn around right now.

   Keep those dots handy. The next time you handle the item, stick another dot on it. Do this every time you have to pick it up, even if just to move it out of the way to get at something else. You'll get mighty sick of sticking those dots. And you'll create a vivid visual testimony to the amount of time you spend managing the clutter.

   If seeing is believing, you will be committed to applying steps 1 through 5 even more rigorously. It will also prompt you to question yourself every time you feel the impulse to make a photocopy, print out an e-mail, clip an article, or save a schedule. It's difficult enough to manage the paperwork others generate—don't be your own biggest offender.

Getting back to diets . . . keeping in shape is a lot easier than getting back in shape. Deflect the incoming and manage the day to day so that clutter never again becomes a time-consuming problem.

Quick Fix

Put your paper on a maintenance diet by performing routine cleanup and reducing the amount of paper that comes in.

Organizing Your Work Space

It doesn't matter whether you work out of a converted barn or a high-rise, city-view office: your work space needs to be organized. Again, "organization" does not necessarily mean neat and tidy. What could be organized for you may look to another as if it were struck by a tornado. The important thing is to know exactly where to find anything at any given moment and to have some kind of ordered system set up.

You can go about this any number of ways. Use a modified system of whatever methods your office uses. Apply the same logic (as in what files are a subset of what) to your hard files as you do on your computer system. Whatever works for you is best, of course. Keep in mind, however, that if others need access to your files, the more they can find on their own, the less they'll need to interrupt you.

If you have a system in mind already, get that geared up to go. If there are systems you either use at home or have used in the past, try to incorporate the best of their elements. Remember: The more familiar the system, the easier it will be to stick with it. Tailor your system to your individual needs for that very reason.

As with a diet or fitness plan, your time management system has to work with both your personal and professional responsibilities. Consider the time you'd waste working so hard to incorporate a time management system into your life, only to disregard it a few weeks down the line. At the same time, you must be patient with yourself. Like delegating, implementing new systems will require a greater time commitment at the outset, but will save you, and your associates or staff, time moving forward.

Quick Fix

Don't skimp on ergonomics. If you spend a lot of time at the computer, invest in a good chair that will help your posture and productivity.

Speed Writing

The term *writer* may not appear in your job description, but odds are you're a professional writer. You may not write books or even annual reports or business plans. You probably do, however, write memos, letters, work orders, directions, equipment orders, job evaluations, responses to job evaluations, and resumes and engage in a lot of other exercises that require putting marks on paper or screen so they'll make the sense you intend for a reader.

Confrontation with the blank screen may consistently frustrate you—writing the various memos and reports your job requires is torture. You hate doing them, and you know you don't always do a very good job on them.

Unlike folks for whom "writer" is the primary job designation, you do a lot of other things every day, too. You can't afford to spend a lot of time writing. You also can't afford the time it takes to write and rewrite repeatedly, or to clear up the confusion and misunderstandings that poorly written communication generates.

Write It Right—and Fast

When you write professional communications, you may use a template, or parrot the tone, style, and structure of letters or memos you receive. Often, you'll end up with a stuffy letter that sounds like it was written in a direct marketing campaign. In the worst-case scenario, you may use words or structures that undermine the point of your communication, and the letter will be a waste of your time and worthless to the reader.

Keep it short and simple. The Ten Commandments required fewer than 300 words, and Abe Lincoln needed only 271 for the Gettysburg Address. You ought to be able to get your thoughts down in a couple of hundred words, too, saving your time and the reader's.

For business purposes, writing is functional, not artistic. Avoid excessive use of adjectives and adverbs. For example, rather than "cutting out each and every word that you don't really, really, really need," you can "cut words you don't need," or, better yet, "cut words." Don't say "in order to" if a simple "to" will do.

Eschew obfuscation. Plain talk is always best. Simple, direct language takes less time to compose and less time to understand.

Make your words easy to read by highlighting the main ideas. You can emphasize an idea by:

- Putting it first
- Using underlining, boldface, or larger type
- Breaking a list out from paragraph form with bullets
- Breaking thoughts into separate sections with subtitles

Always emphasize any action you've taken that affects your coworkers, and be clear in stating your expectations regarding any response you need from them.

Get off to a flying start. Formal outlines are a waste of time. If you need to organize your thoughts before you write, create a bubble outline. Identify your subject and write it in the center of a sheet of paper. Put down the major points you want to make, without regard to their order or relationship. Attach reminders about data, anecdotes, and examples you'll want to use. Circle the main ideas and number them in the order you want them to appear.

If you need more information, you'll discover that now (rather than halfway through the project). When you're ready to go, you'll know exactly where you're going.

Now engage in a little flash typing. Just let the words fly, without worrying about punctuation, spelling, or sentence structure. Capture the essence of each idea and how the ideas relate to each other.

You'll need to go back and edit, of course, but the time it takes to flash-type a rough (very rough) draft and then edit it will be less—probably much less—than it would be to push your way along, word by tortured word, trying to create perfection as you go.

On the off chance you don't know how to type fluently, or if you have trouble composing on the keyboard, and if your work life entails significant amounts of writing, you will save yourself both time and frustration by learning to touch type. Get accustomed to composing on the keyboard. It may feel unnatural at first, but you'll soon learn how to let the thoughts flow from your brain to your fingertips.

Sustain the flow. Take breaks before you need them. Writing is one of the most tiring things you can do while sitting down. Don't wait until you're exhausted. Stretch, take a walk, get some water, and return to the battle refreshed.

Don't wait until you're stuck before you stop, either for a break or at the end of a day's session. If you leave feeling frustrated or stumped, you'll carry a sense of dread around with you. Once you force yourself to sit down and get back to work, you'll have a tough time getting started.

Even if you take a break knowing exactly how you'll continue, you should jot yourself a few notes on the next two or three points you want to make. You'll be ready to start again without a warm-up.

Finish cleanly. You've said what you needed to say. Now you need to come up with the Big Finish, right? Wrong.

Trying to come up with an important-sounding conclusion is another waste of time. If the piece of writing is long, reiterate the main idea or restate your expectations regarding the next step. If the communication is short, simply end strongly with your final point.

Edit by the numbers. You've written fast and loose—and the writing shows it. You've got some editing to do.

If possible, schedule other work so you can set the still-steaming masterpiece aside and do something else before you go back to revise it. That usually means getting the rough draft done far enough ahead of deadline, and that's a matter of good planning.

Don't microedit until you've macrocut. First, take a realistic look at the document and delete the repetitious, the irrelevant, and the rambling passages.

Now go over whatever remains, using a checklist

of the specific problems you need to look for, including misspellings and dangling modifiers, the almost-but-not-quite-right words, passive voice construction, and vague references. This is also the time to fill in specific data points that previously may have been either estimates or complete blanks.

If possible, have a coworker proof your work. Even if that's not possible, don't even think about sending out unedited work to its intended audience. You'd save a little time up front, maybe, but you'll spend that time and more writing the second and third memos clarifying the first one, holding a meeting to explain what you really meant, or explaining to the boss why your report shouldn't have caused the client to cancel its contract.

Above all, keep in mind that no amount of time or effort will salvage your damaged reputation.

Quick Fix

Like the document you created earlier to remind yourself of mistakes to look for in a project, develop a checklist of writing weaknesses to use when you revise your work—include *your* common spelling and grammatical errors.

chapter seven

Save Time Online

Know Your Resources

The Internet is a powerful tool and resource. People around the world are connected to it and take advantage of its benefits. In addition to the fun and ease of corresponding by e-mail, you can shop, do research, and make reservations online. You can also get directions, look for jobs, and check the news and weather.

If you aren't connected at home or the office, you still have access. Libraries, schools, and businesses such as some office-supply superstores will allow you access, either for free or a small fee. If you don't feel you have any use for the Internet, think again. The Internet provides a wealth of information on pretty much any subject you can imagine. If you need to save time, get online.

Beware of traps, however. Because the Internet offers information on such a wide variety of topics, it is easy to let your curiosity get the best of you. To avoid wasting time on the

Internet, you need to know exactly what you want from it at all times. Be as specific as possible, and don't wander from the page.

The Internet is a worthwhile time management tool only if you use it wisely. It is easy to get distracted by the vast amount of possibilities that it offers. Many people spend hours surfing the Web, chatting online, absorbed in e-mail, and sifting through information. Stay in control of your time and don't get trapped in the Web.

Online Job Search

Finding and securing a job can be a frustrating and draining process, but it is something everyone has had to do at one time or another. You may spend days, months—sometimes even years—searching for the perfect job. Amid the sea of resumes, cover letters, hidden (or missed) opportunities, trips to the post office, and interviews, you may be tempted to just give up or give in and settle for your second (or third) choice.

With advances in technology and communications, job searches have become easier to execute. Of course, looking for a job is always hard work, but the time and energy you put into it will not be so tense, and may be more productive. The Internet has become a popular resource for both job seekers and employers because it facilitates everything from job postings to preparing you for the interview. What used to take days to achieve now takes only minutes.

Today, businesses looking to hire employees take full advantage of the Internet. To stay competitive in the employment pool, you need to be a savvy seeker yourself. You might want to look into job search Web sites where you can post your resume. If you do not have a particular site in mind, go to any search engine and enter key words like "job search" and "auto mechanic" or "patent attorney," and you should get a listing of relevant Web sites. Remember: The more specific you are, the more helpful your search results will be.

In addition to posting your resume on career Web sites, you can go directly to the sites of specific companies you'd like to work for—many now have screen space devoted to employment opportunities. Most newspapers, certainly those in major cities, list the classifieds, as do city sites themselves. All this is available to you in one sitting at the computer. Already, just with the available resources, you have saved yourself a substantial amount of time.

Quick Fix

If you plan on relocating, the Internet will be a valuable job search tool. Through an online connection to the local newspaper, you'll find housing and employment opportunities.

Online Resume

To make the most of your Internet job search, create an Internet-friendly resume. Traditional paper resumes are by no means obsolete; you will still run across leads that require you to mail or fax a resume. However, having an Internet-friendly resume on file will allow you to e-mail your resume straight to a prospective employer or post it on an online database. You can send it out as many times as you like without having to do more than move your fingers.

Although the basic information should remain the same as that on your traditional resume, the formatting may require a bit of reworking to keep your online resume clean, legible, and professional. Use the following suggestions to keep you on track.

- Put your name, and only your name, on the very first line. That may be your format anyway, but it is especially

important for an online resume.
- Do not include any artwork or graphics.
- Set all your text as flush left. And, keep the individual lines fairly short.
- Be careful when using special formatting. Most online resumes print as text-only documents, so italics, bold, and underline features probably won't work. If you want to stress something, put it in all caps.
- Similarly, don't use fancy fonts. Use a common font such as Times New Roman.

E-mailing a Resume

If you choose to send your resume to a company via e-mail, you will need to get a specific e-mail address for the human resources department or for a contact name. (Do not just send your resume to addresses labeled "info" or "webmaster.") Although it looks better to send your resume as an attachment, many companies will automatically delete messages with attachments due to the possibility of catching a virus. Include your resume in the body of the e-mail, then bring hard copies (at least two) of your formal version when you interview.

Online Resume Databases

Proof your resume, and have someone else double-check it; then, go to the online resume databases. The databases will present your resume to recruiters and hiring managers worldwide. Hundreds upon thousands of companies will have access to your very own resume. Try to comprehend how much time, energy, and money you would spend traditionally mailing or even faxing a paper resume to all the companies that have access to the Internet—you've accomplished the same thing with a simple click of a mouse.

How to Submit Your Resume

Decide where you are going to post your resume. Use search engines to pull up any Web sites or newsgroups that pertain to the job or industry that interests you. Several Web sites will not only allow you to post your resume, but will also give you tips on creating a resume, let you search job listings, let you do company research, and even lead you through a mock interview.

Sites usually provide step-by-step instructions on how to submit your resume. Sometimes you will be required to fill in fields such as name and address, others will allow you to just copy and paste your entire resume into a text box. The sites will also give you additional information pertaining to how long your resume will be posted, what to do if you want it removed, and whether there are any fees involved.

When you have your resume all set and ready to go, you can begin the hunt. Even if you have posted your resume for all to see, it is a good idea to conduct your own search. You will waste time just standing by, hoping someone will come to you. Be aggressive. You can't go in for the kill if you haven't begun the hunt!

Travel Made Simple

Planning a vacation? Need a night out on the town? Let the Internet be your guide. Airline, car rental, hotel, and restaurant reservations can be made and confirmed over the Internet just as they are on the phone, but without the holding time.

Planning a Vacation

If you love vacations but dread planning them, the Internet will become a good friend to you. You won't have to go from travel agency to travel agency, haggle about prices over the phone, or go to the bookstore to find information on the place you want to visit. All you need to do is sit down at your computer, have a dream in mind, and type in key words or phrases.

Once you have chosen a destination, it's time for a little research. Whether you want to hand over the project to a travel agent or compile everything yourself, you need not leave the computer to do so. From renting a car to finding the perfect sandals, you can do it all on the Internet.

First, you need to know how you are going to get to your destination. Does it make more sense to fly or drive? Even if you are taking a cruise, you need to figure out how to get to the boat.

Flying

If you are planning on flying, there are several sites available to you. In addition to the individual airline companies' sites, you can find discounted fares by searching for "airline tickets." Compare prices, check flight availability, pick your days and times of flight, choose seats, hold a reservation, book a flight, purchase your tickets, have your tickets mailed to you or electronically processed, confirm your reservation, and check flight schedules. You don't have to repeatedly call the airline for information, wait on hold while someone finds answers to your questions, or go through a series of voice-mail menus. Just type in what you want and let the Internet do the rest.

Driving

If you are planning to drive, use the Internet to get the information you need. For instance, do you want to rent a car? Hundreds of businesses online are just waiting to serve you. Shop around to find the best deal in your area. You can get price information, choose the type of car you want, and make your reservation.

Once you arrange for your vehicle, you are going to need to know how to get where you are going. Search for "driving directions" to find Web sites that can give you directions to your destination. Type in your starting address and the destination address, and the site will draw you a map, lay out step-by-step directions, and give you an estimated timetable. Print them out and get ready to hit the road. Some sites will also offer to locate hotels and restaurants along your route so you can make prior reservations easily.

Lodgings

Do you want a city hotel, a national chain, just one night near the airport, or a bed and breakfast for a weekend getaway? The more you know, the easier your search will be.

If you have accumulated points for a free night with your favorite chain, go directly to that company's Web site for information. Or, if you want to conduct a broader search, look for "Boston hotels" or "Napa Valley bed and breakfasts." Like renting a car or making airline reservations, getting your accommodations settled and confirmed can all happen online.

Do Your Homework

Now that you are satisfied that you will arrive safely, you may want to do a little homework on the place you are visiting. If it is a foreign country, you will probably want to check out the native customs so you don't embarrass yourself and your home country. Plus, you will be much more relaxed if you know a bit about your surroundings.

Conduct a search of your destination for timesaving information. If you have a good idea of the area, you will know beforehand what you want to see and where you want to go. Find the opening and closing times of points of interest, tour-ticket prices, and even bargain deals not available to everyone. You may even want to create a schedule according to the information you find on the Internet.

Quick Fix

If you plan on visiting a particular destination often, you may want to invest in a guidebook. Online guides, however, will provide a great overview to help you get oriented to a new city or region while you try to plan your itinerary. Look for "travel guides," then enter your destination.

One-Stop Shopping

How much time do you spend shopping? Driving to and from the stores? Even when you know what you want, how long does it take to find what you need among the endless aisles and racks? What about in the checkout line? A shopping excursion can be an all-day job. But it doesn't have to be.

Think of the Internet as the "world wide mall." Most major businesses, and even quite a few small ones, now offer their services online. Thousands of stores offer hundreds of thousands of products. What do you need? It is all but guaranteed that you will be able to find it on the Internet. Even most of your favorite catalogs probably have Web sites.

Online Education

Although online education is not new, it may not be for everyone. It is, however, worth investigating if your schedule, an extended illness, or other circumstances prevent you from committing to attending classes the old-fashioned way.

Online classes have all the same attributes as a traditional class, except that the classroom is a Web site. They have qualified instructors, textbooks, assignments, deadlines, class discussions, tests, grades, and college credit. The difference is that you can participate in the class as it fits into your schedule and from the comfort of your own home. This allows you to get the education you want without having to stress out about the effects it will have on your time management system.

Are you interested yet? Even if the idea of going back to school doesn't really appeal to you at this time, you may decide you want to take a class in the future, and the Internet may be the best route to take.

How to Sign Up for an Online Class

Most schools will require you to apply to the program. Visit a school's Web site and look into its Web page on distance learning or online education. Once you decide that the institution offers what you want, carefully read over the admission guidelines. The school will have an application you can fill out and submit right online.

Once you are accepted, you can begin to choose the courses you would like to take. Even though this is an easy process and the Internet makes taking classes convenient for you, don't get carried away. Remember that this is a real class for real credit. Don't take on more than your schedule will allow, and budget time to complete necessary schoolwork.

How Online Classes Function

Each school is different and will provide you with the necessary information you'll need on its procedures. Most classes will begin and end along the traditional class schedule. Generally, there aren't specific times in which you need to be "in class." You can log on to your class at pretty much any time of day. (Sometimes, however, you will be unable to log on due to system maintenance.)

As with conventional classes, online classes often require textbooks. You can order them directly through the school's online bookstore, or you can choose to order them elsewhere online. Chances are, you still will not have to move from your comfortable chair.

A qualified instructor will generally lead the class in all basic forms of learning—lectures, assignments, discussions, and tests. However, lectures will be read, not heard, and discussions are typed, not voiced.

Assignments have deadlines attached, so don't think you can stretch the class out over a period of years. Assignments will often need to be downloaded, and you can return them to the instructor via e-mail.

Discussions, often in the form of chat rooms, e-mail, or message boards, will take place regularly. Because of the freedom to participate in class at times convenient to you, you may not always get a response to a question right away. Everyone in the class is on a different schedule, so don't get impatient with the pace of the discussion. Sometimes instructors will set up specific times for the entire class to sign in to a chat room so everyone can bounce ideas off of each other and get an immediate response.

Tests will be administered. This is usually the one time you are required to be logged on during specific days or even hours. Because the tests are normally timed, this part of the class requires a bit more structure.

You will then get a grade and, assuming you pass, college credit. This is the same credit you would have received had you sat in the physical classroom on specified days at specified times. And look at all the time you've saved. By taking an online course, you've cut out the time it would have taken to get ready for class, commute to and from class, and rearrange your schedule to make room for the set class times.

Just these benefits alone should get you excited about going back to school. But before you dive right in there, review your personal goals and your schedule. If school isn't a priority, don't bump another priority out of the way to make room for it.

chapter eight

Values-Based Time Management

What *Do* You Want?

A recent survey asked Americans to list the most important elements in their lives. The number listed next to each item indicates the percentage of people surveyed who listed it among their top three priorities.

Priority	Percentage
Family life	68%
Spiritual life	46%
Health	44%
Financial situation	25%
Job	23%
Romantic life	18%
Leisure time	14%
Home	11%

If you aren't spending enough time on the three elements you've listed as your most important priorities, consider the following:

1. You misrepresented your priorities.
2. You aren't putting your time where your heart is.

Quality Time

As stay-at-home parents joined their partners in having less and less time for their children, and for each other, the theory of *quality time* was born. If you have quality time, then a little bit of very good time together will compensate for the lack of lots of just okay time together.

In reality, quality time is a myth. Instead of quality time, families simply have less time, and what time they do have is pressure time. Relationships can't be scheduled; they just happen.

Meaningful moments, breakthrough conversations, and wonderful gestures occur in the midst of everyday business, often when you least expect them. If you aren't spending time with your loved one, you're going to miss many of the casual moments, and you'll be putting a heavy burden on the time you do have together.

Personal Prioritizing

You may say that your family, health, and spiritual life are top priorities, but you aren't spending much time on them. Could you be wrong about your own priorities?

The process of writing a list of priorities is different from the process of living your life. Your list could reflect the things you think *should* be most important, or things you *wish* had a stronger presence in your life. If your priority is to make a big pot of money, then say so and go for it. If your priority is to eat, drink, and be merry, then that's okay, too. You can't prioritize realistically until you know what's important to you right now; keep in mind that, like everything, your priorities will change over time.

Time Is Money

You aren't just working for entertainment centers and sporty cars. You're working to feed and clothe your children, and to keep a roof over their heads. You're working so the government won't have to take care of you. You're working so you'll be self-sufficient even when you're too old to work.

Work is not only what you do to occupy yourself, it's the effort that is paid back in music lessons, sports camp, family vacations, and saving for your future and your children's education. It's responsible and fulfilling, but no one wants to see his or her little girl run off to college without remembering the first time she toddled across the floor.

The majority of most people's waking time involves some aspect of work, whether it's commuting, odd hours, or being sequestered in your home office. But if you're lucky, your vocation may also be an avocation—a passion, even—that will help you grow professionally and intellectually. Maybe your profession even incorporates your health, or your spirituality, fulfilling several of your priorities at once.

Hard Work

Knowing exactly how to "have a good family life" or to "be healthy" can be a lot harder than going to the office and churning out reports. Not only is the process itself vague, at best, but the results are intangible and often slow in coming.

On the other hand, jobs are defined by explicit tasks or quantified expectations. They aren't always easy, and they aren't always pleasant, but at least they're usually clear. You probably know what you're supposed to do; you probably have a good idea of what it's supposed to look like. And if you don't have even that much to go on, you can be sure that at the end of the day, there is someone who will tell you whether you've succeeded.

When will you know that you've been a good child or parent, friend or spouse? How will you know? What about your health? What about your overall quality of life? Only you can honestly judge your priorities and whether you live the life you really want, but you do need to be honest with yourself.

Quick Fix

When considering you personal priorities, go back to the Important versus Urgent question. Your priorities will change over time; just be aware of them.

The Values-Centered Life

So, like many, you're a time-pressured individual without enough hours in your day for the important things in life. So now what? What can you do to make time to tend to your family, health, and spirit? One big do-it-yourself project . . .

Create a Personal Mission Statement

Business and organizations have them, even if the employees or members are unaware of it. The mission statement is not policies and procedures (though those may be included). The statement describes what the organization wants to be, and what it wants to accomplish. Ideally, every member of the organization should contribute to building the statement, then work to embody it.

What is your mission in life? Why are you living? What do you hope to be and do with your life? What values and assumptions form the foundation of your mission? Spend some time with these questions. Let them sink in, and review them again and again. Like your priorities, your answers will change as you and your life do.

Get Behind It

Once you've at least identified where you are, consider the next questions: How will you act on your beliefs? How will your life reflect your values? What will you do to fulfill your mission?

If family life is a top priority, be committed to it. It may mean working only fifty-hour weeks so you can go to Little League games *and* garden with your spouse. It may mean forfeiting the new car in order to make the kitchen bigger so you can all help at once. Maybe it's just leaving your work at the office so that when you come home, your mind is right there with your body.

Your career could be your priority. So you've cut down on socializing, you skip the gym, and you bring work home. If what you do is important to you—because it supports your other values (social work) or interests (graphic design)—then you are consciously choosing to live your values.

Put It on the Schedule

Some things are more conducive to scheduling than others, and between bringing work home and not doing it because you haven't read to your child in a week, penciling in a run might be the last thing on your mind.

There are commitments you make to yourself, however, that only you can manage. Exercise, photography classes, and yoga are just a few. Volunteering, choir practice, and therapy are some others. As important as these aspects of your life—the active definitions of your values—are, they will not become urgent until you write them down, in ink.

Put it on the day planner. Be as conscientious about keeping that appointment as you would be about an audience with the president or a quarterly evaluation with the boss.

Go Gently

As you seek to change the way you live, prepare yourself: all change, including change in personal habits, is stressful.

Old habits are hard to break, and daily life patterns are the most deeply ingrained habits of all. You're also going to be overpowered by life at times, no matter how carefully you've planned and how well you've anticipated.

Don't berate yourself. Gently remind yourself and do differently next time. Slowly, the new way will become the "right" way, the "natural" way. Give yourself credit for what you do. If you finish fifteen of the seventeen items on your to-do list, rejoice in what you've done. Do one thing at a time, with all of your energy, your attention, and your heart. Finally, with all the planning, evaluating, and scheduling, don't try to do too much.

chapter nine

Beating Stress

Stressless—Is That Even a Word?

Stress is your body's reaction to the demands placed on it. There are several types of stress—some bad, some good, some annoying, some fatal. How you deal with stress can mean the difference between good and bad. If you are having difficulty managing your time, you undoubtedly have a problem with stress. If you're making efforts to manage your time, you should also do what you can to manage your stress level.

Stress is a constant. It doesn't go away, and it doesn't just show up haphazardly. Only when your stress level gets out of control do you begin to feel its effects. As soon as you realize that you are actually stressed all the time, you will be able to differentiate between the types and effects of stress.

Effective Stress Management

The causes of stress vary, depending on your lifestyle. The keys to effective stress management are:

1. **Identifying the source.** What causes stress on your body? Does it have a positive or negative effect?
2. **Taking inventory.** Do the stress producers outweigh the stress reducers?
3. **Adjusting to achieve balance.** You aren't powerless—create a balance between the stress producers and the stress reducers.
4. **Maintaining methods of healthy living.** Learn how to reduce the negative stress on your body to live a healthy and relaxed life.

Before you dive headfirst into this process, stop and think about what a significant impact stress has on your life. You may think it is just an annoyance that gets you down once in a while, but in reality, it can have severe effects that you may not be aware of. If you thought about skipping out on this chapter, think again.

Potential Physical Effects of Stress

- Rapid heart rate
- Muscle tension
- An increase in blood pressure
- A change in sleeping patterns
- Dizziness
- Nausea
- Fatigue
- Back pain
- Rapid breathing
- Headaches
- Clammy skin
- Rashes

Health Problems Linked to High Stress

- Heart disease
- High blood pressure
- Diabetes
- Sexual dysfunction

- Stroke
- Weight problems
- Digestive problems
- Ulcers

Potential Psychological/Emotional Effects of Stress

- Nightmares
- Low self-esteem
- Lack of concentration
- An increase in nervousness
- Irritability
- Anxiety disorder
- Forgetfulness
- An increase in the use of drugs and alcohol
- Depression
- Anger

Now reconsider the seriousness of stress. Good time management will help you to reduce your stress level somewhat, but there are other actions to take. The following sections will take you step-by-step through getting your stress level under control.

Take Stock

Look at the activity log you kept at the beginning of the book. Consider your feelings and reactions to each of the activities that took place. Did any of them make you feel nervous, panicked, anxious, eager, rushed, or confused? Did you have any physical ailments that accompanied these actions? What was your reaction to the completion of the activity? Take note of those that heightened your stress level. Write them down and try to determine the length of time they caused you to feel stressed. If the stress outlives the activity, it may be time to look again at your priorities and debate whether or not the particular activity has any true bearing on your life.

If remembering your reaction to these activities is difficult, start recording your responses to them in a diary or journal. Reflect on your feelings and attitudes toward everything you do. It doesn't necessarily have to be a physical action you take, it could be a thought or feeling that stimulates you. This is a time for self-awareness and should be taken seriously. Granted, it will take some time and effort on your part, but the results are well worth it. Your health and performance may be at risk.

Remember: Stress isn't always negative. Don't overlook those activities that bring you pleasure and a sense of accomplishment, although they are also stress producers. However, this type of stress yields positive consequences. If at all possible, identify every source of stress, good and bad.

Eliminating all stress isn't possible, so identify activities that caused the greatest change in your stress level, focusing on those that are recurring (quarterly performance review) or ongoing (adjusting to a new baby). You will learn to reduce the negative effects of these stress producers, thereby reducing your overall stress level.

Stress Less

Now that you have a good idea of what causes your stress, what relieves it? Refer back to your activity log. Did any of your actions remedy the effects of stressful situations? How did you handle them? How did you react upon completion of those tasks? In order for your stress level to even out, you need to create a balance between the stress producers and the stress reducers.

If you still don't have a good idea of how to relieve stress, picture yourself completely relaxed. What is it you see? Are you lying down? Reading a book? Refusing to stifle that yawn? Participating in enjoyable activities also reduces the negative effects of stress—you don't have to be passive to be relaxed. Whatever works to ease your body and mind is a stress reducer.

If you are like most people, your stress producers will outweigh the reducers. Although there are little things that can be done to lower your stress level, such as stretching or taking a deep breath, it's likely that the completion of one activity kicks off the start of a new one. Going from one activity or task directly to another only compounds stress. If you don't allow yourself a break, tension will rule your life on a day-to-day basis.

Adjust to Achieve Balance

Okay, so stress isn't going to go away; what can you do about it? How do you achieve the balance that is so important for your physical and mental well-being?

Bring out your priority list! Focusing on what is important will allow you to spend less time on the trivial things that have a tendency to grate on your nerves. Try to put everything you do into perspective. If it doesn't take up a lot of space in the big picture (or *your* big picture), it doesn't warrant considerable stress.

Eliminate as many stress producers as possible. For instance, if driving in morning traffic sets your teeth on edge, consider public transportation. Or, if that isn't an option, inquire if anyone would be interested in carpooling. Try a different, less popular route to escape the crowds.

Make stress reducers a part of your schedule. Take breaks often, even if they are only two minutes long. Those two minutes will do you a world of good in the long run. If a warm bath relaxes you, make it a part of your routine. Stretch frequently if you are working diligently for an extended period of time. Don't give the stress time to make it to your muscles.

While you can't control every aspect of your life, there are several ways you can get around the amount of stress placed on you. Be creative; do something out of the ordinary. The important thing is to make the proper adjustments, whether in attitude or action, to balance the producers with the reducers.

Maintain Methods of Healthy Living

There are several ways you can curb the negative effects of stress. If you can't eliminate the stress, don't feel powerless. You can still live a healthy and happy life. The following are some suggestions to help you deal with stress affirmatively.

Eat well. This isn't to say a nice chunk of chocolate once in a while is going to ruin all your efforts for stress management. But keep in mind that a healthy life is a happy life.

Get enough sleep. With a good night's sleep you will wake refreshed and ready to take on the world. Stress will have a harder time worming its way into your day if you are well rested.

Exercise. It is good for you not only physically but also emotionally. Physical exertion helps you get out pent-up frustrations and tension. Plus, if you are physically fit, you will feel better about your appearance, which, in turn, increases your self-esteem.

Don't take life too seriously. Have fun and laugh. Laughter is the best medicine, after all.

Don't stifle your emotions. If you keep your emotions bottled up, never allowing them to surface, the pressure will become so great you will eventually explode.

Let go. Don't worry about things that are beyond your control. Unnecessary worry creates unnecessary anxiety. You are also likely to adopt an overall feeling of helplessness, which may spill over into your other activities.

Use (healthy) escapism in moderation. Don't go overboard and run away from your problems, but it helps to take a step back once in a while to try to get an objective view of the situation. Take a drive in the country or a walk in the park to clear your head before trying to tackle a difficult situation again.

Maintain a positive attitude. Don't expect the worst or you may very well make it happen.

Reward yourself.

Set Up a Routine

While some people will be bored to tears at just the thought of a routine, others live their lives by one. Just like habits, routines can be good and bad. They can greatly benefit your management of time, but they can also hinder it. Where do you draw the line? When is a routine in your best interests, and when will it drag you down?

Examine your life and see what routines, if any, you already have set up. For instance, you may wake up at the same time every day, put on a pot of coffee, shower, eat, brush your teeth, and so forth. A routine doesn't have to be every day, though. It may occur once a week or once a month. If you do the same activities in the same order on a regular basis, you have yourself a routine. Now, do you want the good news or the bad news first?

Pros

There are several advantages to using a routine. A routine becomes a habit, and habits require little prior thought. Your morning routine does not require you to stop and think about what you are going to do once you wake up or after you shower or after you eat. The sequence of actions is established; you simply go through the motions. So you save yourself the time not only of thinking, but also of making a decision.

Routines are easy to schedule. If an activity is completed on a regular basis, you will have a pretty good idea of how long it is going to take you. Even though your estimates of time are often up in the air, your routine should be quite an educated guess. You know how much time to allow yourself to get ready for work in the morning because it is something you do every day.

Other people can schedule around you more easily if they are aware of your routines. Often, it is difficult to make schedules mesh. If you have a routine that will not falter, however, another person can easily find areas in his or her own schedule that will complement yours.

Routines provide a sense of safety and comfort. If you don't have to wonder what is going to happen minute by minute, your stress level will not be nearly as high. Even though the rest of your schedule and surroundings may be chaotic and disorganized, you will find peace in the comfort zone of your routine.

Cons

Although routines have several benefits, they can overload your schedule. You should not schedule one routine right after another to fill your whole day. If you schedule for routines, make sure they are dispersed throughout the day. Thinking that you can live your life according to one big schedule is unrealistic. Unexpected events are sure to occur, leaving you unprepared and defenseless. However, if you are aware of the unforeseen possibilities, you will at least be mentally, if not physically, prepared.

Believe it or not, routines can actually affect your self-esteem, and not always in a positive way. Routines create a comfort zone. Comfort has its place in a hectic life, but you cannot hide out in your comfort zone. You will eventually create a box around yourself that separates you from the world, rendering yourself incapable of dealing with any other interaction. Your self-esteem will plummet, as will your time management and your overall quality of life.

Good Routines

If you aren't sure where to draw that line, consider some of the following ideas for tasks that work well within a routine:

- Taking your medicine or vitamins at the same time every day
- Walking your dog during specified times throughout the day
- Making one (and only one) trip to the post office every week
- Reviewing your priorities and goals at the end of the month
- Exercising

Suit Yourself

Now you have an idea of what you should and shouldn't do with your time. Take a look at your schedule. Does it incorporate your values and your priorities? Do your routines help or hinder you? Does delegating add or reduce stress? Use what you've learned about yourself and apply the elements that are most helpful; remember that moderation and balance are fundamental aspects of a low-stress, healthy, and productive lifestyle.

Quick Fix

Time management isn't about maximizing the number of items you can check off in a day or a lifetime. It's about living fully, productively, joyfully—by your definition of these terms.

index

a

activities
   assigning value to, 36–37
   identifying stress causing,
     107–8
activity log, 37–38
approval seeking behavior, 55

b

breaks
   scheduling, 23
   tracking, 15
business writing, 83–87
busywork, 61–62

c

Caller ID, 58
classes, online, 96–98
clutter
   See also paper flow
   controlling, 79–80

d

databases, resume, 92–93
daydreaming, 43
decisions
   handling mistaken, 72–73
   indecision and making,
     66–69
   standing by, 71–72
   sticking to, 60
   tips for making, 70–71
delegation
   advantages of, 47
   hang-ups, 49–50
   process, 48–49
desktop organization, 76
   See also work space
     organization
distractions
   See also interruptions
   about, 42
   controlling, 43–44
   cost of, 44

phone calls, 57–59
welcome, 42–43
driving information, 94–95

e
education, online, 96–98
80/20 Rule, 35–38
e-mail, of resumes, 92
ergonomics, 83
errors
eliminating, 72–73
fear of, 69
exercise, 110
expendability, fear of, 55
external time, 3–4, 9

f
filing tips, 77–79
flight information, 94
future, 4

g
goal setting, 23–24
guilt syndrome, 55

h
healthy living techniques,
110–11

i
ignorance, fear of, 68–69

indecision
See also decisions
reasons behind, 67–69
as time waster, 66–67
indispensability, myth of, 55
internal time, 2–3, 9
Internet
benefits of, 89–90
classes on, 96–98
job search, 90–93
resumes, 91–93
shopping, 96
travel planning, 93–96
interruptions
See also distractions
limiting, 45–46
responding to, 51–56

j
job search, online, 90–93

l
lateness, perpetual, 7–8
leisure time, 6–7
lists
not-to-do, 24–25
to-do. *See* to-do lists
lodging information, 95

m
mail. *See* paper flow
management issues

cutting down on meetings, 56–57, 63–66

dealing with staff, 61–64

decision making, 67–72

overcoming indecision, 66–72

meetings

cutting down on, 56–57, 63–66

guidelines for, 65–66

preparing for, 64–65

mission statement, personal, 102–4

mistakes

eliminating, 72–73

handling, 72

multitasking

cons of, 40–41

costs of, 41–42

pros of, 38–40

n

negative feedback, 69

notebook, 75–76

o

online

education, 96–98

job search, 90–93

resume, 91–93

shopping, 96

travel planning, 93–96

organization

desktop, 76

work space, 75–83

p

paper flow

controlling, 75–79

dealing with incoming, 80–82

filing tips for, 77–79

getting rid of unneeded, 77–78

sorting, 76–77

speed writing and, 83–87

Pareto's Principal, 35–38

past, 4

people management

handling interruptions, 51–56

saying no, 60

of staff, 61–64

periodicals, 81

personal mission statement, 102–4

personal priorities, 100–2

phone calls

managing time spent on, 57–59

responding to unexpected, 51–54

present, 4

priorities

survey of top, 99–100

establishing, 17–18

important vs. urgent, 27–31
personal, 100–2
to-do list for, 19–27
trivial vs. essential, 30–31
values and setting, 102–4
want/need question and, 31–33

q
quality time, 100

r
reading, 78
resume, online, 91–93
routines, 111–13

s
salespeople, 59
scheduling
  breaks, 23
  goals, 23–24
  time estimations in, 16, 27
shopping online, 96
sleep, 110
speed writing, 83–87
staff
  managing, 61–64
  meetings. *See* meetings
stress
  about, 105
  effects of, 106–7
  healthy living for
    management of, 110–11

identifying causes of, 107–8
multitasking and, 41
reducers, 108–9
reducing, 108–9
routines for management of,
  111–13

t
tardiness, 7–8
technology, using
  productively, 62
telemarketers, 59
telephone calls
  managing time spent on,
    57–59
  responding to unexpected,
    51–54
time
  attitude toward, 4–9
  disregard for, 8–9
  as enemy, 5–6
  estimations, 16, 27
  external, 3–4, 9
  internal, 2–3, 9
  lateness and, 7–8
  leisure, 6–7
  log, 12–15
  making, 33–34
  quality, 100
  tracking use of, 12–15
  work, 7, 101–2
  your relationship with, 1–2,
    9–12

time management
    80/20 Rule and, 35–38
    allowing for interruptions
        in, 15–17
    effective systems for, 9–12
    reasons for difficulties in,
        9–12, 33
    setbacks, 10–11
    on the telephone, 51–54,
        57–59
    values-based, 99–104
    your relationship with time
        and, 9–12
to-do lists
    creating healthy, 20–24
    difficult, 19–20
    important vs. urgent items
        on, 27–30
    not-to-dos on, 24–25
    poorly prepared, 25
    preparing, 26–27
    prioritizing your, 27–33
    trivial vs. essential items on,
        30–31
travel planning, online, 93–96

u
uncertainty, 67–68

v
vacation planning, online, 93–96
value scale, 36–37

values-centered life, 102–4
voice mail, 58

w
work space organization
    clutter control, 79–80
    paper management, 75–82
    tips for, 82–83
work time, 7, 101–2
Wright, Jan Benson, 55
writing
    editing your, 86–87
    speed, 83–87